TALES FROM HOLLYWOOD

also by Christopher Hampton

plays

WHEN DID YOU LAST SEE MY MOTHER?

TOTAL ECLIPSE

THE PHILANTHROPIST

SAVAGES

TREATS

ABLE'S WILL: A Play for Television

THE PORTAGE TO SAN CRISTOBAL OF A.H.
(adapted from the novel by George Steiner)

translations

Molière's DON JUAN

Ödön von Horváth's

TALES FROM THE VIENNA WOODS

Ödön von Horváth's

DON JUAN COMES BACK FROM THE WAR

Henrik Ibsen's THE WILD DUCK

TALES FROM HOLLYWOOD

CHRISTOPHER HAMPTON

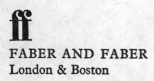

FABER AND FABER
London & Boston

First published in 1983
by Faber and Faber Limited
3 Queen Square London WC1N 3AU
Printed in Great Britain by
Latimer Trend & Company Ltd Plymouth

Library of Congress Cataloging in Publication Data

Hampton, Christopher, 1946–
  Tales from Hollywood.

  I. Title.
PR6058.A555T3 1983   822'.914   82–25154
ISBN 0–571–11883–6 (pbk.)

British Library Cataloguing in Publication Data

Hampton, Christopher, 1946–
  Tales from Hollywood.
  I. Title
  822'.914   PR6058.A555

ISBN 0–571–11883–6

CHARACTERS

In the play:

ÖDÖN VON HORVÁTH
CHARLES MONEY
THOMAS MANN
HEINRICH MANN
HELEN SCHWARTZ
NELLY MANN
SALKA VIERTEL
MARTA FEUCHTWANGER
BERTOLT BRECHT
HELENE WEIGEL
HAL
ANGEL
JACOB LOMAKHIN
ART NICELY

A YOUNG MAN
KATJA MANN
LION FEUCHTWANGER
TONI SPUHLER
WALTER

*And with the friendly
participation of:*
JOHNNY WEISSMULLER
CHICO MARX
HARPO MARX
GRETA GARBO

In memory of
DAVID MERCER

Tales from Hollywood was originally commissioned
and produced by the Center Theater Group at the
Mark Taper Forum, Los Angeles, California
(Artistic Director: Gordon Davidson). The play
was first performed in Great Britain at the
National Theatre in 1983.

Ödön von Horváth (b. 1901) was one of the most
talented writers of his generation. He was killed on
1 June 1938, in a freak accident on the Champs-
Élysées, when a branch of the chestnut tree under
which he was sheltering fell on his head.

A colleague, Walter Mehring, who was staying in the
same hotel in Paris, went into Horváth's room. On his
desk were two half-empty glasses of red wine and a
page of notes for the novel (*Adieu Europa*) Horváth
was just starting to write. The first line of the notes
read: 'Ein Poet emigriert nach Amerika. . . .'

INTRODUCTION

A word about the origins of this play seems necessary, if only to acknowledge the contribution of those without whose help and active support it would never have existed. At the beginning of 1980, I decided to stop concentrating on writing for the cinema, an enjoyable but in my case apparently fruitless pastime, and return to the theatre, where, for various reasons, I had not worked for some years. As I was sifting alternative subjects, I was telephoned by Kenneth Brecher, the Associate Director of the Mark Taper Forum Theater in Los Angeles, where, a few years earlier, I had worked on a revised version of my play *Savages*. He explained that the theatre was running a scheme under which, at regular intervals, they were commissioning a series of plays set in Los Angeles and invited me to write one; and of the potential subjects he then listed, there was one which immediately caught my interest: the European émigrés and refugees from Fascism. However, as I had never accepted a commission in this way before, I asked if it would be possible for me to come and explore for a couple of weeks before I made up my mind. He agreed.

So it was, in the course of ten days in May, that I discovered the riches of the special collections in the library at UCLA; conceived the idea, during a meal in Chinatown with Kenneth Brecher and Gerald Turbow, who teaches a course on the émigrés in California, of making Ödön von Horváth my central character; met Marta Feuchtwanger, widow of the novelist Lion Feuchtwanger, a sprightly lady in her early nineties with almost total recall, who was to become by far the single most important source of information for the play; and attended a party in Santa Monica, at the house which once belonged to Salka Viertel (in which scenes 6 and 16 of the play are set) and which now belongs to Gordon Davidson, the Artistic Director of the Mark Taper, who was to direct the play—a party to which Gordon had invited as many of the surviving émigrés and those involved with them as he had been able to contact.

Over the next two years the Mark Taper paid me an advance, found me a house, part-financed a stay of ten weeks in 1981 (when I wrote the play) and another of six weeks in 1982 (when we rehearsed it), provided me with a series of assistants, traced documents and posted them, made contact with people I wanted to interview (and even some I didn't) and eventually gave the play a lavish production in March 1982. It will be seen, then, that my gratitude to Gordon Davidson, Kenneth Brecher, William Wingate and their staffs must be considerable: I don't know if the play they summoned into existence was exactly what they had in mind—but it could certainly have never been written without them.

* * *

I need, in addition, to thank various institutions, writers and individuals, who, wittingly or otherwise, helped while I was writing the play. The Schönberg Institute, under its very friendly director, Leonard Stein, made its library available; the Institute of Germanic Studies in London was the scene of furtive jubilation, as yellowing literary magazines and obscure newspaper polemics yielded up their secrets; the London Library was as reliable as ever; and the very helpful staff of the Special Collections at UCLA pointed me towards the Oral History Program, a wonderful anthology of reminiscences, transcribed from tape, the shining jewel of which is the 1,750-page interview with Marta Feuchtwanger, which, supplemented by her own shrewd observations during our conversations, is the principal source for the play.

Rather than give a full bibliography, I want simply to indicate those writings which were most useful to me. On Horváth, there is Traugott Krischke's indispensable biography *Ödön von Horváth, Kind seiner Zeit*; on Heinrich Mann, his autobiography, *Ein Zeitalter Wird Besichtigt*, among his many novels *Ein Ernstes Leben*, and a thesis by Robert Marshall Stanford: 'The

8

Patriot in Exile'; on Thomas Mann, his own letters and diaries (which rather uncannily confirmed, after I had finished the play, that he *had* stayed at the Beverly Hills Hotel in 1938) and his book about the writing of *Doctor Faustus*, *The Genesis of a Novel*; on Nelly Mann, Joachim Seyppel's novel *Abschied von Europa* and a controversy between him and Golo Mann conducted in the columns of *Die Zeit* in February 1973; and on Brecht, his collection of screenplays (*Texte für Film*), his riveting two-volume diary of the period, the *Arbeitsjournal*, Klaus Völker's biography, Martin Esslin's book *Brecht: a Choice of Evils* and James K. Lyon's study *Bertolt Brecht in America*. On the feelings of the émigrés in general, I found the most evocative writings were those of Alfred Döblin, Lion Feuchtwanger, Leonhard Frank, Hermann Kesten, Erika and Klaus Mann, Alfred Polgar and Carl Zuckmayer. Two other books I should particularly mention are Nigel Hamilton's *The Brothers Mann*, which I had read with great fascination before this commission and which was therefore in my mind throughout the project; and Salka Viertel's autobiography *The Kindness of Strangers*. I also had three films run for me: Fritz Lang's *Hangmen Also Die* (for information) and Josef von Sternberg's *The Blue Angel* and Billy Wilder's *Sunset Boulevard* (for pleasure): the influence of these last two films on the play will not be lost on those who know them.

Finally, I want to thank the following for their help and encouragement: Margaret Camplejohn; the late Harold Clurman, who talked to me in New York about Brecht, when he was already very ill; Helen Deutsch; Janet Emmons; my wife Laura for her typing and cooking skills, which are considerable, and my children Alice and Mary for their adaptability; Philip Himberg; John Houseman; Bronislau Kaper, the composer and wit; Gene Kelly; Jane Kramer; Norman Lloyd, who was especially supportive and whose account of the rehearsals of *Galileo* was unforgettably vivid; Lindsay Nelson; Nancy Olsen; Eleanore Tanin; John Russell Taylor, who generously allowed me to read the proofs of his comprehensive and fascinating account of the émigrés in California, *Strangers in Paradise*; Gerald Turbow, who was involved from the very outset; the late King Vidor; Billy Wilder, who gave me a hugely entertaining morning; and Fritz Zweig, the conductor.

I have already indicated the indispensability of Marta Feuchtwanger's contribution to the play, but not perhaps the trouble she took to be helpful or the support she gave throughout, which was of crucial value to me. And I must end by thanking my assistant, Clark Hansen, who dug up obscure books in out-of-the-way libraries, came up with copies of films at short notice, drove literally thousands of miles, finally taking over as my driver when my own uncertain flirtation with the automobile broke down, and generally cut months off the writing time. I had never before had an assistant whilst writing a play: thanks to Clark, I find it hard to envisage managing without one in the future.

C. H.
January 1983

ACT ONE
1938–41

ONE

A curious rippling submarine light.
Into it steps a striking figure: fortyish, somewhat overweight, overcoat open to display a well-cut, double-breasted, grey flannel suit, a Homburg on his head and black shoes, good but scuffed, on his feet, his exophthalmia the most notable feature of his expressive face.
He pauses a moment, assessing the audience.

HORVÁTH: Hello. My name is Ödön von Horváth. (*Pause.*) Ödön. (*Pause.*) No, Ödön. (*Pause.*) Oh, never mind, call me Ed. (*Silence. He listens.*)
No, that's all right, don't apologize. There's no reason you should ever have heard of me. I had a certain reputation about ten years ago. You know, in the theatre. In Germany. I was considered, you know that word, when they don't really like you but think you might not go away, promising. I had a play in rehearsal when the Nazis came in. It never opened. After that, no one would put on my plays in Germany, however bad I tried to make them. In the end, I took to writing novels. Also . . . but you don't want to hear about all that and I don't want to tell you. Just that through all those years to be a writer in Germany was to be a non-swimmer in the water-polo team.
(*He moves a few paces, listening. Distant thunder. The underwater effect vanishes and he seems now to be standing under an old-fashioned street light.*)
During the thirties, which were also, as it happened, my thirties, I travelled a good deal. I knew the melancholy of

11

railway stations and the grey wallpaper of cheap hotels. And as the decade, which appeared to have been constructed by a dramatist of the kind many of my more progressive contemporaries were denouncing as hopelessly old-fashioned, as it moved by way of smoothly plotted climaxes and neatly engineered last-minute reversals towards its inevitable conclusion, a good many of us, us German writers, I mean, had very narrow escapes. I want to start by telling you about mine. So.

(*He pauses. Very distant thunder. A light wind, rising.*)

I never had subscribed to the fashionable view that the cinema as an art form could not survive the coming of sound. On the other hand, I hadn't yet had sufficient experience of the medium to realize that the writer's importance to it was somewhere on a par with the hairdresser's. Consequently, when I was invited to Paris in May, 1938, to discuss filming one of my novels, I accepted at once. I was still unfamiliar enough with the business to be surprised when at the first meeting, instead of discussing the project, I was bundled into a car, driven to the Champs-Élysées, handed a ticket and sent in to see the latest sensation: *Snow White and the Seven Dwarfs*. Hard to tell what connection it might have had with my novel (which dealt with Nazi education policy) and, given the historical circumstances, I found the film a little optimistic in tone; all the same, in many ways a remarkable piece of work, don't you agree? Afterwards, we had our meeting, which lasted a good ten minutes, at a sidewalk café, and then Siodmak's wife offered to drive me back to my hotel. It was a pleasant evening. I said I would walk.

(*He sets off, strolling across the stage, humming 'Hi ho, hi ho, it's off to work we go.' The wind gets up. A few premonitory drops of rain and then the sound of a solid downpour.* HORVÁTH *turns up the collar of his coat.*)

However, I was only halfway down the hill when, out of a clear blue sky, this storm.

(*He's about to hurry on, when a light comes up on a* YOUNG MAN, *standing in the shadow of an overhanging branch. He's*

12

*strikingly Aryan in appearance, his hair almost platinum. We
see the glint of his glasses, the shabbiness of his raincoat, and, as
he beckons to* HORVÁTH, *the dull and surprising gleam of an
incongruous pair of black leather gloves.* HORVÁTH *hesitates,
then shakes his head politely. Loud thunderclap.* HORVÁTH
starts and moves quickly over to join the YOUNG MAN. *He has
to raise his voice, against the sound of the wind, lashing
through the trees.*)

I joined him in the shelter of an enormous chestnut tree,
opposite the Théâtre Marigny. Even before he spoke I
sensed that he might be, like me, a foreigner and when he
did speak, in better French than I could muster, of the
weather, the whereabouts of the nearest bar and the
unbearable vulgarity of the Arc de Triomphe, I began to
think he might even be a fellow writer. But before I could
ask him, a bizarre commotion occurred.

(*We hear the sounds, as he describes them.*)

Some way off from where we were standing, a tree suddenly
snapped in the wind. This fell against our tree, causing a
thick branch above our heads to detach itself from the
trunk with a slight sucking noise. It then landed on the
back of my companion's head.

(*Without a sound, the* YOUNG MAN *falls to his knees. Then he
topples forward on to his face. The back of his head, which is
in full light, is crushed like an eggshell. Silence falls, abruptly.*)

He died instantaneously. And this was the incident which
prompted me to make the following remark: Why is it
people are so afraid of the Nazis? Why aren't they afraid
just walking down the street?

(*Lights snap out on the* YOUNG MAN. HORVÁTH *moves
downstage, reflecting for a moment before speaking.*)

I know of no political theory or philosophical system which
takes into account the workings of chance. I don't just
mean a few centimetres to left or right and it would have
been me face down on the stone: I mean that chance, in its
most brutal guise, was about to take charge of the lives of
millions of Europeans. Not that people realized, of course—
I have friends who took taxis to the internment camps. For

me, the tree on the Champs-Élysées was enough. And being, as I was, a German-speaking Hungarian born in an Italian town now part of Yugoslavia, or, as it might be, a native of the sea coast of Illyria, chance was on my side. Not only did I have a Hungarian passport, I even had a real American uncle, in Lexington, Virginia, who came across right away with the famous affidavit. So while some scrambled desperately for papers which might take them to Mexico City, Helsinki, Shanghai, anywhere, and others sat serenely in Switzerland, while some, calmly or in panic, took their places in the cattle trucks or swallowed poison in obscure border towns, I was already, flushed with optimism and disregarding certain superstitions I have concerning water, well on the way to . . .

(*Projection: the skyline of New York.*)

Even as I marvelled, though, standing on the deck at dawn, I became aware of a difficulty. For I was a man who, for complicated reasons which took the form of simple fear, was unable to step into an elevator.

(*The projection fades. Birdsong.*)

Lexington, Virginia, was no better. For my uncle, although in other respects most amiable, was a radio ham and also a member of the *Bund*. So every evening was spent grappling with the bloody cat's whisker in order to get the full benefit of the Führer's latest thinking.

(*Brief snatch of a Hitler speech, varying wildly in volume and drowned in static.*)

It seemed there was only one thing for it. Namely . . . (*He spreads out his arms.*) Los Angeles!

(*Immediate blaze of white light: circus lighting.* HORVÁTH *begins to wander offstage.*)

Chugging across interminable wheat fields, I dreamed of legendary encounters.

(*He's gone. But on the stage, sitting in a wicker chair, wearing a white jacket and a panama hat, glasses and a moustache dyed black, is a man of about sixty-five. He is reading. Quietly in the background, a little Wagner plays, the prelude to* Lohengrin. *A moment passes. Then the tranquillity is rudely shattered by a*

*familiar, ear-splitting cry. The man looks up to see, crossing
the stage in a great arc, hanging on the end of a rope, a
startling apparition:* TARZAN. *Completing his cry, he lands at
the man's feet. The man looks up at him, his mild expression
touched with apprehension and annoyance.* TARZAN *stretches
out his hand. The man reluctantly accepts it.*)

TARZAN: Me Johnny Weissmuller, you Thomas Mann.

(*The Wagner snaps out. Cross fade and lights up on* CHICO *and*
HARPO MARX. HARPO *is in baggy white trousers and carries a
tennis racquet.*)

CHICO: Who wuza this little guy you wuza playin tennis with?

(HARPO *shakes his head; disconsolate expression.*)

He beat you, uh?

(HARPO *nods, tearful.*)

Who wuz he?

(HARPO *draws his racquet, which has a motor horn on the end
of it, across an imaginary violin.*)

Heifetz?

(HARPO *drops to one knee: his sneakers have no toecaps. He
counts out silently; six toes to each foot.*)

What?

(*Same routine.*)

He gotta twelve toes? No wunna he beat you. What's his
name?

(HARPO *works his jaw furiously.* CHICO, *puzzled. As the
excitement of the question-and-answer session mounts,* HARPO
punctuates it with blasts on the motor horn.)

Teeth?

(HARPO *shakes his head.*)

Moosejaw?

(HARPO *shakes his head. His jaw now working frantically, he
takes an imaginary something out of his mouth and sticks it
behind his ear.*)

Chewinagum?

(HARPO *nods: then shakes his head. Continuing to chew, he
begins to flap imaginary wings.*)

Ostrich?

(HARPO *shakes his head: begins to move around the stage*

15

chewing and flapping his wings.)

Chicklet?

(*He's pleased with this, but* HARPO *shakes his head, exhibiting terrible frustration; redoubles his efforts.*)

Chewinaboid?

(HARPO *nods, delighted: congratulatory blasts on the horn.* CHICO, *however, is puzzled again.*)

Chewinaboid? Chewinaboid? I don't know no Chewinaboid.

(HARPO *holds up a finger for silence. Then, magically, he strums on his tennis racquet the four regular, melancholy, opening notes of 'Verklärte Nacht'.* CHICO's *expression clears.*)

Ah! Arnold Schoenberg!

(HARPO *nods ecstatically.*)

Why didn't you say so inna the foist place?

(HARPO *frowns.* CHICO *throws an arm round him and begins to lead him offstage.*)

You gotta be careful with him, he gotta very sneaky rhythm.

(*As they leave the stage,* HORVÁTH *enters, arm-in-arm with a staggeringly beautiful woman:* GRETA GARBO. *He's now dressed for California. They advance downstage, looking deep into each other's eyes. Suddenly, a flashbulb pops. Then, the flashes of what must be dozens of cameras.* GARBO *breaks away from* HORVÁTH, *holding up a hand. The flashbulbs stop.*)

GARBO: Ve vant to be alone.

(*The flashbulbs start up again. She turns, looks at* HORVÁTH *for a moment, then runs offstage, distraught.* HORVÁTH *looks after her, sadly. The lights change to normal California daytime.* HORVÁTH *smiles.*)

HORVÁTH: Well. Thomas Mann did know Johnny Weissmuller. Schoenberg did play tennis with Harpo Marx. And I did meet Garbo. But I need hardly say the reality was very different.

TWO

Sitting behind a desk innocent of books, but with a great many tele-phones deployed around it, is a shortish, overweight man of middle years: CHARLES MONEY. *He looks up as* HORVÁTH *is shown into his office.*

In the scenes where he is with other émigrés, or simply addressing the audience, HORVÁTH *has no accent. However, in his scenes with Americans, his accent is very strong, and although it will improve as time passes and the play goes on, as will his use of English, it will always remain very noticeable in these scenes.*

MONEY *struggles to his feet, extending a plump hand.*

MONEY: Hi.
 (HORVÁTH *shakes his hand, bowing slightly.*)
HORVÁTH: Mr Money.
MONEY: Chuck.
 (HORVÁTH *looks around uncertainly, not at all sure what he means by this.*)
 Good of you to find the time, Mr Horváth.
 (*He mispronounces the name horrendously.* HORVÁTH *winces.*)
HORVÁTH: Ödön.
MONEY: Uh?
HORVÁTH: Ed.
MONEY: Oh, yeah, good.
 (*The phone rings.* MONEY *sinks behind his desk, selects a receiver.*)
 I'm in a meeting. Oh, Christ, all right.
 (*He gestures to* HORVÁTH.)
 Ed. Sit.
 (*Then, effusively, into the receiver*) Jack! How are you!
 (HORVÁTH *sits.*)
 End of next week, Jack, I told you . . . Yes, I know that, but . . .
 (*Silence, during which* MONEY *puts his hand over the receiver.*)
 Talking to this guy is like drowning in cold gravy. (*Back into the receiver*) Well, I really appreciate your patience on this, Jack . . . She's fine. How's Eileen? . . . Yeah, nice talking to you.
 (*He puts the receiver down, a trace shaken.*)
 Have you seen *The Adventures of Robin Hood*?
HORVÁTH: This is a film?

17

MONEY: You haven't seen *The Adventures of Robin Hood*?

HORVÁTH: No.

(*A different phone rings.* MONEY *picks up the receiver. Brief silence.*)

MONEY: Of course it's raining. I can see it's fuckn raining!

(*He slams down the receiver, irate, takes a moment to collect himself.*)

You worked for Fox over in Europe, is that right, Ed?

HORVÁTH: Yes.

MONEY: And my people tell me you wrote a play about Edward the Second.

HORVÁTH: Please?

MONEY: Play. Theatre play. You wrote a play. About Edward Second. English king.

HORVÁTH: No.

MONEY: No?

HORVÁTH: No.

MONEY: Oh.

(*Silence.*)

HORVÁTH: Ah, I know that, what you mean. *Eduard der Zweite.* Yes. No. This play was from Bertolt Brecht und Lion Feuchtwanger.

MONEY: You didn't have anything to do with it?

HORVÁTH: No.

(MONEY *considers for a moment.*)

MONEY: Either of them in town, you happen to know?

HORVÁTH: No. Mr Feuchtwanger is in France and Mr Brecht is, I think, in Denmark or so.

MONEY: But you are familiar with the material?

HORVÁTH: Sorry? My English.

MONEY: Do you know the play?

HORVÁTH: Oh. Yes. But in any case is it an old English play.

MONEY: What's that?

HORVÁTH: Yes. From Christopher Marlowe.

(*Silence.* MONEY *broods.*)

And I don't think he is in town either.

(*No reaction to this from* MONEY, *who continues to reflect, frowning.*)

MONEY: Let me have it run for you.

HORVÁTH: I'm sorry?

MONEY: *The Adventures of Robin Hood.* It was huge. It did three million domestic. It'll give you an idea.

HORVÁTH: For what?

MONEY: Listen, let me explain. These things nobody can explain. But for some reason right now English history is very hot. So somebody came up with this Edward the Second idea, and what we have here is a treatment.

(*He hands* HORVÁTH *a slim folder.*)

HORVÁTH: Thank you.

MONEY: It's a way of presenting the facts we think may work, but you don't have to take any notice of it, hell, you're the writer.

HORVÁTH: Yes.

(MONEY *frowns.*)

MONEY: You a member of the Screenwriters' Guild?

HORVÁTH: No. You want I become a membership?

MONEY: No, no, that's fine.

(*Silence.* MONEY *stares at him for a moment.*)

OK, Ed, I'm prepared to offer you a hundred dollars a week.

(HORVÁTH *makes a gesture, wearily assenting.*)

Half now, half on delivery.

HORVÁTH: But . . .?

MONEY: You need two weeks?

HORVÁTH: Maybe.

MONEY: OK, you got it. End of next week, then.

(*He smiles. Then a thought strikes him and the smile disappears.*)

You OK to write in English?

HORVÁTH: Oh, sure. I am taking lessons.

MONEY: Good.

HORVÁTH: Yes. I am now knowing three thousand words of English.

MONEY: Congratulations.

HORVÁTH: Excuse me?

(*A telephone rings.* MONEY *selects a receiver, listens.* HORVÁTH *turns to the audience, rises and moves downstage. His accent*

has disappeared. In the background, the lights go down on MONEY, *as he listens on the phone.*)
The telephone. They even have some damned bird out here sounds like a telephone.

That week, Hitler marched into Czechoslovakia. *Variety* said: Hitler's reshuffling of Central Europe represents a loss of $2\frac{1}{2}$ to 3 per cent of total foreign film income.

THREE

HORVÁTH: These mundane tasks were interrupted by a summons to Parnassus. The Nobel Prize winner was passing through on one of his lecture tours, speaking on 'The Problems of Freedom' or somesuch burning topic. I had, of course, met Thomas Mann often during the twenties, in Germany, but this was the first evening I ever spent with him alone.
(*Lights up on* THOMAS MANN, *comfortably installed in his bungalow at the Beverly Hills Hotel, pouring himself a cup of coffee.* HORVÁTH *joins him, picking up a glass of brandy on his way.*)
Pleasant as it was to be able to speak my own language again, the occasion was not without its mishaps.
(THOMAS MANN *lights a cigarette, carefully.*)

THOMAS: What did you think of my lecture? Be honest.

HORVÁTH: I shall have to be very honest: I'm afraid I missed it.

THOMAS: Oh?

HORVÁTH: I have a deadline coming up, my first American screenplay.

THOMAS: I hope I'm not keeping you from it now.

HORVÁTH: Also, I wasn't quite sure if I would be able to follow your English.

THOMAS: My English is very good.

HORVÁTH: Oh, yes, it's mine that's terrible. I took some lessons in Vienna but I had to give them up.

THOMAS: Why?

HORVÁTH: They made me feel like a head waiter.

(THOMAS MANN *relaxes, somewhat mollified.*)

THOMAS: What does it deal with, this screenplay of yours?

HORVÁTH: Edward the Second of England. Based on Marlowe's play.

THOMAS: Interesting. Did you ever see Brecht's version?

HORVÁTH: No.

THOMAS: Oh, I did. About fifteen years ago in Berlin. I remember it vividly. It was dreadful.

HORVÁTH: In what way?

THOMAS: Everything so relentlessly ugly. Costumes made out of old sacks. They kept complaining about the king's extravagance, and then on he'd come wearing something they'd just shaken the potatoes out of. Even the king's boyfriend was the most unattractive lump in the company. And quite deliberately so. I don't begin to understand that Brecht, do you? Of course, as you know, in my book *Buddenbrooks* the dentist is called Herr Brecht, so I've never been able to take him quite seriously. His name doesn't have the right resonance. I feel much more comfortable with your work.

HORVÁTH: Well . . .

THOMAS: That first charming little book of yours, you know the one I mean, I thought it was remarkable. No one else has been able to write like that about life inside the Third Reich. How did you manage to find out all those things?

HORVÁTH: I . . . I've kept up my contacts with people inside Germany.

THOMAS: Well, so have we all. But I couldn't write about what it is to live there. You're very bold.

HORVÁTH: Well, you know, I . . . at the beginning, I went back quite often.

THOMAS: Really?

HORVÁTH: Oh, yes, I even, I meant to tell you this, at the book-burning, the great book-burning in Berlin, I was there.

THOMAS: I don't see how you could possibly have been.

HORVÁTH: I saw them all filing past Goebbels in their academic robes, heaving books on to the bonfire, and that professor, what's his name, Bäumler, I saw him dance. I heard him shouting, 'Burn, Thomas Mann, burn!', yelling like a bad actor.

(*Silence*. THOMAS MANN *is shaken*.)

HORVÁTH: Then Goebbels made a speech and said: 'Tonight, the intellect awakes.' I watched the whole thing.

THOMAS: Weren't they burning your books too?

HORVÁTH: No, no, I'm not well-known enough. The compensations of obscurity.

THOMAS: It's true. Fame carries very heavy obligations.

HORVATH: I'm sure.

THOMAS: I often wonder, you know, if we writers have done enough to prevent the world from rolling to the brink of war.

HORVÁTH: Oh, my family has a very poor record when it comes to preventing wars. My father, who was a diplomat, had a meeting with the Archduke Franz Ferdinand in the spring of 1914. His Highness said he was planning a tour of Bosnia. My father assured him this was an excellent idea and particularly recommended a visit to Sarajevo. So all this is really his fault.

THOMAS: Forgive me if I can't bring myself to smile. Ever since that monster destroyed Czechoslovakia . . . my brother Heinrich and I are Czech citizens now, you know, the government granted us special passports. I blame perfidious Albion, of course. How can that cretinous weakling Chamberlain suppose that letting Hitler do as he pleases is less dangerous than negotiating with the Communists? If he'd stood firm, none of this would ever have happened, Hitler would have fallen . . . and I would not have been placed in the intolerable position of having to advocate war. That's enough of that. Have you a new book ready for us?

HORVÁTH: Yes. It's called *Europe, Goodbye*.

THOMAS: Will you read some of it to me? Do you have it with you?

HORVÁTH: No. No, I don't.

THOMAS: Oh, what a disappointment.

(*Silence*. THOMAS MANN *seems to be waiting for something*.)

HORVÁTH: Perhaps . . . would you read something of yours?

THOMAS: Well, all right, if you insist, certainly. My voice is a little tired from lecturing, but . . .

HORVÁTH: Well, then, please don't . . .

THOMAS: No, no, if you insist.

(*He fetches a thick manuscript from a nearby table.*)

At the moment, I'm writing about Goethe. This was intended to be a *Novelle*, but these things have a habit of expanding out of my grasp. I don't have your enviable gift of brevity any more.

HORVÁTH: Some would say I'm short-winded.

THOMAS: Oh, come, come. Now, where are we?

(*He shuffles through the manuscript.*)

Of course, at this critical point of history, it may seem criminally irresponsible to spend one's energies painting a portrait of some long-dead German writer, however great . . .

(*Pause.* THOMAS MANN *waits.*)

HORVÁTH: Oh, I don't see why.

THOMAS: But one must obey the dictates of one's instinct. It takes years for the secret significance of a work of art to reveal itself to the artist himself, let alone to his public.

HORVÁTH: Well, I must say your story *Death in Venice* has taken on a special meaning for me in recent years.

THOMAS: No doubt on the grounds of its convenient length.

HORVÁTH: No. No. Not on those grounds.

THOMAS: I started work, for instance, on my *Joseph* book in '23. Who could have imagined then how relevant the theme of an intellectual in exile would become? The laws of art are truly unfathomable. We have no choice but to obey them, even if we can never understand them.

(*He picks up the manuscript again, puts on his glasses.* HORVÁTH *turns to address the audience.*)

HORVÁTH: I agreed that the laws of art were whatever it was he'd said they were. He began to read.

(*He rises and begins to move downstage. The lights on* THOMAS MANN *fade slowly to black.*)

He read from his imperishable masterpiece, *Lotte in Weimar*.

But the sinuous elaboration of his syntax, the lulling
sonorities of his laureate's voice were such that, regrettably,
within a very few minutes, I was sound asleep.

. . .

FOUR

HORVÁTH: I delivered my script and was asked to call back the
following day. Only the kind collaboration of Christopher
Marlowe had enabled me, in the time allotted, to complete a
piece of work in a foreign language. I made the play as
filmic as I could, but almost all the words were Marlowe's.
I returned, quietly confident.
(*Lights up on* CHARLES MONEY's *office.* MONEY *sits glowering
behind his desk.* HORVÁTH *approaches, smiling.*)
Mr Money.
(MONEY *rises and picks up a heavy black folder, which he
instantly hurls across the room at* HORVÁTH. *They look at each
other for a moment.* HORVÁTH's *expression is quizzical.
Suddenly,* MONEY *shouts at him.*)

MONEY: Whaddya think that is?
(*Silence.* HORVÁTH *picks up the folder and studies it briefly.*)

HORVÁTH: Well, heavens to Betsy, it's my script.

MONEY: Script! You wouldn't get that on fuckn radio!
(*Silence.* MONEY *paces up and down.* HORVÁTH *watches him
with mild interest.*)
How could you do this to me, Ed?

HORVÁTH: Do what?

MONEY: I put my ass on the line for you. Have you any idea
what kind of trouble I'm in now?

HORVÁTH: No.

MONEY: Well, now, Ed, this is going to be a very short meeting.
But you're new in town and I think I'd better straighten
you out.

HORVÁTH: Am I bent?
(*A phone rings before* MONEY *can answer. He picks up the
receiver and shouts into it.*)

MONEY: No! Five minutes!

    (*He slams the receiver down, looks up at* HORVÁTH.)

    Listen, Ed, I know your English is bad, you can't help that, but this is a goddam disaster area.

HORVÁTH: Well, I used the Marlowe . . .

MONEY: I don't care if you used fuckn Webster's, Ed, English this ain't.

HORVÁTH: I see.

MONEY: Another thing. You can't even type right. The whole script is laid out like some goddam poem.

HORVÁTH: You want me, that I explain . . .

MONEY: No, I don't want you, that you explain. All I'm saying is, you want Ty Power and Linda Darnell to read your script, you don't bring them fuckn *Hiawatha*.

HORVÁTH: This I understand.

    (MONEY'*s tone changes abruptly to one of solicitude.*)

MONEY: I gave you a treatment, Ed. Why didn't you work from the treatment?

HORVÁTH: Excuse me?

MONEY: The treatment!

HORVÁTH: Oh. Yes, I threw this away. I thought it was unbelievable wulgar.

MONEY: Vulgar! Wait a minute, Ed, I wrote that.

    (HORVÁTH *shrugs.* MONEY'*s rage is mounting again.*)

    Vulgar! Listen, when I read your script, I pass over the fact it was in pidgin English, there was this stuff, I couldn't believe it, I had to go back and read it again, but there it was, I've never seen anything like it in the script of a major motion picture, in your story the King of England is a goddam faggot!

HORVÁTH: A faggot?

MONEY: A faggot, a fruit, a . . . homosexual!

HORVÁTH: Ah. But this is historic true.

MONEY: Are you crazy? So what? Listen, for all I know Robin Hood liked to do it with sheep, you think anyone wants to see that? This is for family audiences, not for the back room of the cathouse. This is an adventure picture, not the goddam ballet. You come to me with some piece of shit has the King of England climbing into bed with a boy and you tell me I'm vulgar? Jesus fucking Christ!

HORVÁTH: So I am how you say fired.

MONEY: You bet your ass.

HORVÁTH: Then I say good day.

(MONEY *calms down as* HORVÁTH *starts to leave.*)

MONEY: Wait a minute.

(HORVÁTH *waits.*)

I don't know what you do in Europe, Ed, I don't know the kind of material Fox goes for over there. All I'm telling you is you can't pull this kind of stunt in this country. We're not ready for it.

(*A phone rings.* MONEY *picks up the receiver angrily.*)

Didn't you hear what I said? . . . Oh . . . oh, Jack . . . Yeah, listen, I have a little problem . . .

(*As he speaks,* HORVÁTH *gets up again and leaves the room. Lights down on* MONEY, *as* HORVÁTH *approaches the audience.*)

HORVÁTH: I couldn't find it in my heart to be too angry with Herr Money. Later on, of course, I realized what had really been happening: he was a writer-producer, and he'd subcontracted me, at a fraction of his own salary, to do a job he was supposed to be doing himself. Anyway, at least he paid me, despite his horror at European morals, which is more than I can say for some later employers, however amiable their manner. So. First blood to Hollywood.

FIVE

HORVÁTH: I had earned a reasonable amount of money in my youth, but all of it had disappeared on train fares and hotel rooms, in bars and taxi cabs and coffee houses. Now I discovered, that in contrast to many parts of Europe, this was a country in which it was difficult to be poor with dignity. However, the inconveniences I suffered were as nothing compared to those of my friends who were still in Europe. The governments of Britain and France, entirely ignoring the misgivings of *Variety*, had declared war on Germany. Individuals in America were making heroic efforts to help those trapped in Occupied Europe, but at the same time chance was sharpening the knives on its chariot wheels. The man the State Department put in charge of the refugee problem was a former Ambassador to Rome who had been enormously impressed by the punctuality of Mussolini's trains, and who thought anyone who mismanaged their life to the extent of becoming a refugee was deeply suspicious, probably undesirable and, as often as not, a Jew.

I, on the other hand, was a beneficiary of all this frenzied activity. An organization was formed, called the European Film Fund, to provide work in Hollywood for needy émigré writers. And so it was that I found myself an employee of:

(*Projection: The Warner Brothers logo; music: signature tune from* Looney Tunes.)

Truth to tell, when it came to devising something for all their new writers to do, the Brothers found themselves somewhat at a loss. So, the corridors of the writers' building were jammed with bewildered Germans asking each other how they ought to be treating their secretaries.

(*Lights up on a corner of the Warner Brothers commissary. Also, way upstage and not in light, is the indistinct figure of an old man:* HEINRICH MANN, *slightly hunched, waiting, as if lost or abandoned, not moving. In the commissary, sitting alone at a corner table, reading, drinking black coffee, is a slight, dark woman in her late twenties:* HELEN SCHWARTZ.)

One day, in the rest room, I was amazed to find, standing next to me, Heinrich Mann, Thomas Mann's elder brother. As he had always been something of a hero of mine, I invited him to join me in the commissary for a coffee.

(*He moves upstage to collect the old man;* HEINRICH MANN *is sixty-nine, a dignified figure, somewhat heavier in build than his brother, but with the same neat moustache and round glasses. His clothes are old but good, incongruously formal for the setting, a handkerchief carefully arranged in his breast*

pocket. He moves with HORVÁTH *into the commissary.* HELEN
looks up when they arrive, then back at her book. HEINRICH
installs himself at a table. HORVÁTH *moves upstage, returning
immediately with coffee on a tray. As he's unloading the tray,
he's staring at* HELEN. *She looks up and sees him. Instead of
turning away, he smiles at her. She nods in brusque
acknowledgement, frowning slightly.* HORVÁTH *sits down next to*
HEINRICH, *who's just taking a sip of coffee.*)

HEINRICH: Not coffee as we think of it, of course, but then in
France, these last few months, it wasn't to be found
anywhere.

HORVÁTH: Hard to imagine France without coffee.

HEINRICH: I would have been happy to spend the rest of my life
in France.

(*Silence.*)

Tell me, what is it they expect us to do here?

HORVÁTH: Keep out of their way, I think, I don't know.

HEINRICH: But we're supposed to be writing scenarios, is that
right?

HORVÁTH: Theoretically.

HEINRICH: What are scenarios?

HORVÁTH: Oh, stories you think might work well as films.

HEINRICH: People keep asking me to go to, what are they called,
the film shows here?

HORVÁTH: Screenings.

HEINRICH: Screenings, yes, and I sit and watch them, but I
never know why they ask me.

HORVÁTH: They want to know what you think of them.

HEINRICH: Oh, I always say the same thing. Very good.

HORVÁTH: Even if they're terrible?

HEINRICH: Yes. Unless they're completely terrible.

HORVÁTH: Then what do you say?

HEINRICH: I say very interesting.

HORVÁTH: I don't think you need my advice.

HEINRICH: They always introduce me as the man who wrote
The Blue Angel.

HORVÁTH: Ah, yes.

HEINRICH: At first, I used to say, I didn't write it, I wrote a

28

novel thirty-five years ago, on which the film is very loosely based. They changed the ending, I would say. Then I understood they didn't want to hear that. So now I say, did you like it oh I'm so glad thank you very much.

HORVÁTH: I'm sure you're right.

HEINRICH: Yes. My entire American reputation stands on the legs of Marlene Dietrich.

HORVÁTH: Surely not.

HEINRICH: When I arrived in New York last month with my nephew Golo, the *New York Times* welcomed the arrival of the famous German author, Golo Mann. Then they said he was accompanied by his Uncle Heinrich.

HORVÁTH: I can't believe it.

HEINRICH: I wouldn't mind so much, except Golo's never written a book in his life.

(*Silence.*)

HORVÁTH: If I were you, I wouldn't take any notice of all this, I'd just sit in my office and get on with my novel. You are writing a novel?

HEINRICH: Yes. I am. Is that what you do?

HORVÁTH: That's what I do.

(HEINRICH *nods, digesting this advice.* HORVÁTH *looks across at* HELEN. *Silence.*)

How did you get out of France?

HEINRICH: With extreme difficulty I think is the answer to that.

(*Pause.*)

I had the papers for America and the Spanish visa and the Portuguese visa, but I couldn't get the French to give me an exit visa.

Finally, there was this wonderful young American who said if I didn't go now, I'd be arrested and sent back to Germany. He took us to the Spanish border and we climbed out of France, over the Pyrenees.

HORVÁTH: How did you manage?

HEINRICH: I'll never know. I didn't mind the walking, but I kept falling over. If it hadn't been for Nelly, my wife, I'd still be there. . . .

(*Pause. He looks at* HORVÁTH.)

You must meet Nelly, she doesn't get a chance to see many people her own age, all my friends are so ancient now.

HORVÁTH: I'd like to.

HEINRICH: I don't know how, but she managed to get us tickets on a Greek ship, she fought for them like a wild thing, the last Greek ship out of Europe before Mussolini invaded Greece.

(*Pause.*)

Lisbon harbour, you know. I'm a continental European. I've never even been across the Channel. And the harbour. I can't tell you how beautiful it is. Like some long-lost love. To watch it vanish. Hard to bear.

(*Silence. His eyes are misty.*)

My daughter's still there. With her mother, my first wife. I tried everything I knew, but I couldn't get them out of Prague.

(*Silence.* HORVÁTH *struggles for a change of subject, hits on it finally.*)

HORVÁTH: How is your brother?

HEINRICH: Tommy? He's bought some land out at Pacific Palisades. He's having a house built there.

HORVÁTH: He's all right, then?

HEINRICH: Well, his daughter's family was torpedoed a few weeks ago. She and the baby were rescued, thank God, but Tommy's son-in-law was drowned.

(*Silence.* HELEN *gets up and leaves. Despite the gravity of his expression,* HORVÁTH *is unable to prevent himself from watching her as she goes. She catches his eye on the way out.*)

How much are they paying you?

HORVÁTH: Hundred and twenty-five bucks a week.

HEINRICH: Me too. Yes. Me too.

(*Silence.*)

I know what you're thinking, my boy. How is it we've managed to be so lucky?

(HORVÁTH *rises to his feet and moves downstage. Behind him, the lights fade on* HEINRICH MANN.)

HORVÁTH: That wasn't at all what I was thinking. I was thinking that after the First World War, Heinrich was the most famous writer in Germany, when Thomas Mann was just a name. I remembered the rumours about their not being on speaking terms all through the twenties, and how in 1929 many of us believed the Nobel Prize had gone to the wrong brother. I was trying to control the sadness and anger I felt at rediscovering my old hero in some Burbank toilet.

SIX

HORVÁTH: By now, we émigrés had a favourite meeting place: a little house in Mabery Road, Santa Monica, which belonged to Garbo's writer, Salka Viertel.

(*Lights slowly up on the long table in the front room of the house; the table is set for dinner and lavishly decorated with flowers and candles. It runs diagonally across the stage and upstage of it is an opening which leads to the kitchen. Milling around, standing close to each other to suggest a confined space, are a number of* GUESTS, *mostly of a certain age, formally dressed for the occasion: these include* SALKA VIERTEL *herself,* THOMAS MANN *and his wife* KATJA, LION FEUCHTWANGER, TONI SPUHLER, *the cook,* WALTER *the butler, and as many others as is feasible. Conspicuous among them, and somehow immediately obviously different from them, is a dazzling blonde woman:* NELLY MANN. *She's forty-three, and she's wearing a red silk blouse, stretched tight across her capacious bosom, and holding a glass of red wine, to which she has frequent recourse.*)

We met here to celebrate Heinrich Mann's seventieth birthday: not actually on his birthday, because on that date Thomas Mann was receiving one of his honorary doctorates, this time at Berkeley. All the same, it was a notable occasion and one I would always remember, if only because it was there I first made the acquaintance of the famous Nelly.

(*By now,* NELLY *is at his elbow. She's somehow acquired a second glass of red wine which she holds out to him.*)

NELLY: Want some?

(HORVÁTH *takes the glass*.)

HORVÁTH: Thank you.

NELLY: It's the real French stuff, I think. God knows where she got hold of it.

HORVÁTH: Prost.

(*He takes a sip.* NELLY *takes a swig.*)

NELLY: Of course, I don't mind the Californian, what do you think?

HORVÁTH: I quite like it.

NELLY: Yes, it's rough and strong, and what more do you need, I always say.

(*She laughs.* HORVÁTH *smiles at her.*)

All this lot are so bloody snobbish about it. What do you do?

HORVÁTH: I'm a writer.

NELLY: You're not.

HORVÁTH: Yes. Ödön Horváth.

NELLY: Bloody Hungarian, by the sound of it.

HORVÁTH: Well, you know, the usual Austro-Hungarian mixture.

NELLY: I am disappointed. When I saw you over here, I said to myself, well, at least I bet he's not a writer.

HORVÁTH: I'm sorry.

NELLY: You don't look like a writer.

HORVÁTH: It's good of you to say so.

NELLY: If anyone'd told me, when I was a young slip working the Kurfürstendamm, I'd finish up other end of the bloody world in bloody California with a lot of bloody writers, I'd have blacked his eye for him.

(*She turns, gesturing lavishly at the table. The others, meanwhile, are taking their places at the discreet urging of* SALKA *and* WALTER.)

Heini doesn't want all this, you know. He's been dreading it for weeks. Who wants a lot of people telling you you're seventy? He knows he's seventy, poor old bugger. Bad enough turning forty, wouldn't you say?

HORVÁTH: Ah, there you have me.

NELLY: Get off!

HORVÁTH: No, I promise you, it's a good few months yet.

(NELLY *snorts sceptically.* WALTER *arrives alongside her,
murmuring, sotto voce, gesturing at the table.*)

NELLY: All right, more wine, is there?

(*She sets off towards the table.* WALTER *hurries off for a bottle
of wine, then intercepts her and pours her another glass.*
HORVÁTH *stays where he is for a moment, watching her. The
others are already placed around the table: in the centre,
facing the audience, is* SALKA VIERTEL, HEINRICH *on her right
and* THOMAS *on her left.* NELLY *is opposite her, next to* LION
FEUCHTWANGER *and* MARTA FEUCHTWANGER *is next to*
HEINRICH.*)

HORVÁTH: I thought she was wonderful.

(*He starts moving towards the table, then stops and turns back
to the audience.*)

After the soup and before the special roast beef she'd been
saving, dear Salka Viertel, our hostess, rose to her feet.
This proved to be a fatal error.

(SALKA *is on her feet, waiting for silence.* HORVÁTH *gets to his
seat which is at the downstage end of the table and sits down.*)

SALKA: I just wanted to say what an honour it is for us to be
holding this little celebration in our house and to propose a
first toast to a great writer: to our beloved Heinrich Mann.

(*Everybody rises, except* HEINRICH: *into the ensuing minute
pause comes* NELLY's *voice, clear as a bell.*)

NELLY: I need some more.

(*Silence.* FEUCHTWANGER *fills* NELLY's *glass. Then everyone
raises his glass to toast* HEINRICH. *Everyone sits.* SALKA *turns
and gestures to* WALTER. WALTER *turns and gestures to the
kitchen. Then, proudly,* TONI SPUHLER *emerges from the
kitchen, bearing the roast. However, as she does so,* THOMAS,
*his back to the kitchen, rises deliberately, fumbling for his
glasses, which he then cautiously adjusts on his nose.* SALKA
gestures to WALTER. WALTER *in turn gestures to* TONI, *who
stops, transfixed.* THOMAS *produces a substantial manuscript
from the inside pocket of his dinner-jacket.* WALTER *gestures
again, more urgently.* TONI *turns and retreats into the kitchen.*
THOMAS *clears his throat.*)

THOMAS: This festive gathering then has finally taken place; and its cause—so moving and worthy a cause!—lies so far in the past, it is almost necessary to remind ourselves of it. The cause, my dear brother, is your seventieth birthday, which took place on March the twenty-seventh, and which we were unable to celebrate earlier. I was at fault for this, or rather my commitments were at fault . . .

(HORVÁTH *turns, as* THOMAS *continues to deliver his speech.*)

HORVÁTH: And on he went, as the beef sizzled and browned, to speak of Goethe and Nietzsche, of liberty and pragmatism and evil, till buttocks stiffened and eyelids drooped.

(HORVÁTH *turns away and* THOMAS's *voice surges back.*)

THOMAS: If genius, dear Heinrich, is foresight, the ability to anticipate, the passionate portrayal of things to come, then your work bears the stamp of genius. And if you have, as I'm sure you do, the organic stamina, your old eyes will see what you predicted in your youth: the fall of a tyrant.

(*He whips off his glasses: applause. He nods minimally in modest response: then sits.* SALKA *gestures to* WALTER. WALTER *gestures to the kitchen. A few seconds pass and then:* TONI *with the roast beef. But: as she crosses the threshold,* HEINRICH *rises to his feet.* TONI *freezes.* HEINRICH *searches his pockets, momentarily at a loss. Desperate pantomime between* SALKA, WALTER *and* TONI, *who finally, puce with rage, returns to the kitchen with the beef.* HEINRICH, *meanwhile, has located his speech.*)

HEINRICH: Thank you. (*He reads:*) Well, my dear brother, as you, in the course of your too kind address, so perceptively remarked . . .

(HORVÁTH *turns to the audience, grinning, and* HEINRICH's *voice disappears.*)

HORVÁTH: Afterwards, somebody explained to me they'd been doing this kind of thing ever since they were fifty. And so, at even greater length, as the beef shrivelled and blackened, Heinrich delivered his measured response.

(*He turns back.* HEINRICH *gives a little formal bow.*)

HEINRICH: . . . then, as indeed it is now. Thank you again. Nelly and I are profoundly grateful.

(*He sits, amid warm applause.* SALKA *gestures to* WALTER.

WALTER *signals to the kitchen. Presently, grim-faced,* TONI *emerges from the kitchen with the beef. She's hardly into the room, when* MARTA FEUCHTWANGER *rises to her feet.* TONI *stops, staring in disbelief. Then she thrusts the beef into* WALTER'*s hands and, bursting into tears, rushes back into the kitchen. After a moment,* WALTER *exits with the beef. Meanwhile,* MARTA, *unaware of all this, has launched into her speech.*)

MARTA: I should like to propose a toast to Nelly Mann, without whom I cannot think that this celebration would be taking place. Her cheerfulness and encouragement during that terrible journey over the Pyrenees will never be forgotten by any of us. So I would like to ask you . . .

(*She breaks off.* NELLY *has risen to her feet and now turns to face the audience, her back to the table. One hand is clenched across her breast, the other is covering her face. Her shoulders are shaking.* MARTA *hurries round to her side, reaches up to pat her on the arm.*)

I'm so sorry, I didn't mean to upset you.

NELLY: Upset me?

(*She breaks off, helpless with laughter. For a moment, she can't speak for laughing. She drops her hands and her blouse comes open, revealing a beautiful embroidered lacy bra.*)

No, Christ, I've been laughing so hard, I've burst me button. (*More peals of uncontrollable laughter. Slight consternation among the* GUESTS. SALKA *rises to her feet to try to calm the situation. Blackout.*)

SEVEN

Spot on HORVÁTH.

HORVÁTH: Well, I continued to work for the Warner Brothers, hoping that none of them would notice me, and sure enough, none of them did. And, in the meantime, I found a new way, which was actually an old way, to improve

35

my English.

(*Spot off. Pause. Then the lights come up on* HELEN SCHWARTZ's *apartment.* HELEN *and* HORVÁTH *lie entwined on the sofa. Silence.*)

HELEN: Lot of American men don't like a girl to earn eight times their salary.

HORVÁTH: This is crazy. A girlfriend who takes me out to dinner and drives me to work, you want that I complain?

HELEN: European men must be different.

HORVÁTH: No. I think this, er . . . *Einstellung* . . .

HELEN: Attitude?

HORVÁTH: Attitude, *ja*, is also common in Europe.

HELEN: Then it must be just you that's different.

HORVÁTH: I'm afraid yes.

HELEN: Actually, this is all highly irregular. As a rule, the two-thousand-dollar-a-week writers don't talk to the thousand-dollar-a-week writers, and the thousand-dollar-a-week writers stick pretty closely together.

HORVÁTH: So you are different also.

HELEN: It's just I'm a nice Jewish girl. I like to have someone to look after.

HORVÁTH: Yes, I have been once married to a Jewish girl.

HELEN: Married?

HORVÁTH: *Ja.*

HELEN: You didn't tell me that.

HORVÁTH: Oh, it was just for the passport.

HELEN: What do you mean?

HORVÁTH: I married Maria to give her the Hungarian passport.

HELEN: Oh, I see. And what happened?

HORVÁTH: She used it and left. Gone with the wind.

HELEN: You been married many other times?

HORVÁTH: Oh, I think once is enough for anyone, don't you?

HELEN: I wouldn't know.

HORVÁTH: You know in the Fu Manchu movies, when he says, I can promise you a beautifully painful and slow, slow death? For me this is called marriage.

HELEN: I see.

(*She disengages from him gently, gets up and crosses the room*
36

to light a cigarette. HORVÁTH *sits up.*)

HORVÁTH: Anyway, women have always been very kind to me.

HELEN: I don't know why that should be.

HORVÁTH: Me neither.

(*She smiles at him. Silence.*)

What is it with these Warner Brothers? I write all these goddam scenarios, no one ever says a word to me.

HELEN: You want me to explain that?

HORVÁTH: Sure.

HELEN: It's what I was saying before.

HORVÁTH: What?

HELEN: First, they really don't like to read. So if they have to read, they're going to read what cost them money. Listen, their thirty-five-hundred-dollar-a-week writers earn more while they're taking a piss than you do all week. So whose scenarios do you think they're going to look at?

HORVÁTH: Yes, but I also am costing them money.

HELEN: That's peanuts, Ed. That's charity. You give a blind musician a dime, you don't expect the Goldberg Variations.

HORVÁTH: OK, but it's costing me time. Ten to five every day and the goddam bus rides, when do I have time to write? My writing?

HELEN: You have a lot of time. You know why? Because no one reads your scenarios. And actually it suits you that way, if the truth be known.

HORVÁTH: I suppose.

HELEN: So why are you complaining?

HORVÁTH: I like to be appreciated.

HELEN: You want them to pay you and appreciate you and shut up, right?

HORVÁTH: I think this is fair, yes. Like any artist.

(*They smile; then* HELEN *looks away.*)

I'm sorry. I know for you this is serious business.

HELEN: Yes, it is.

(*Pause.*)

My folks took me to see *The Jazz Singer* in New York when I was fourteen. I thought it was terrible: God, so

37

sentimental. But I was . . . excited by it, you know? In those days I already knew I wanted to write, but I didn't know what.

HORVÁTH: And this decided you for the movies?

HELEN: No. It just started me thinking. A whole new medium. Infinite possibilities. Probably the first art form since Elizabethan theatre to appeal to every age group and every class. And you can take it out to audiences anywhere in the world. Now I can't imagine writing for anything but the cinema.

HORVÁTH: I understand you theoretic.

HELEN: I know it hasn't happened yet, I know the business is run by greedy opportunists and yes-men and chisellers, but they can't hold out forever. Just look at the progress that's been made in what, not even fifteen years.

HORVÁTH: Yes, but it's too powerful for them ever to listen to ze writers . . .

HELEN: *The, th.*

HORVÁTH: Ach, zis goddam sound. I know what is his answer, St Peter, when I come and say, OK, open ze gates: no, no, *the, the.*
(*She laughs, comes over and sits beside him again and takes his hand.*)

HELEN: I liked your novels so much. I wish I could read your plays. Aren't any of them translated into English?

HORVÁTH: No, I'm sorry, I am not enough famous.

HELEN: What are they like, are they political, or what?

HORVÁTH: No, I think you wouldn't call them political, they don't deal about special . . . *Themen* . . .

HELEN: Issues?

HORVÁTH: No, and not from Marxist ideas, like Brecht.

HELEN: Who?

HORÁTH: Bertolt Brecht, he's a writer, bit older than me. I just write about ordinary people, how bizarre they are. I write about life, as it regrettable is. I write about the poor, the ignorant, about victims of society, women especially. The Left attack always: they say easy pessimism. But they love the people without knowing any people. I know the people,

38

how terrible they are, and still I like them. Also, it turns out, my plays were not enough pessimistic.

HELEN: And what about the Right?

HORVÁTH: Oh, already, before ten years . . .

HELEN: Ten years ago.

HORVÁTH: *Ja*, I was in court for fighting in a bar with Nazis. And when my play *Geschichten aus dem Wienerwald*, er, *Tales from Vienna Wood* was in Berlin premiered, the Nazi critic said, not even an audience of niggers would watch the play without they would protest. I stand by my review.

HELEN: Well, I wish I could read German. My father has family in Germany.

HORVÁTH: Oh? Where?

HELEN: Düsseldorf, I think. They're, you know, cousins, I never met them.

HORVÁTH: And are they still in Germany?

HELEN: Far as I know.

(HORVÁTH *shakes his head dubiously, then looks up and across at* HELEN.)

HORVÁTH: You know something, you're the best-looking playwright I ever met.

HELEN: That's the kind of remark I usually take exception to.

HORVÁTH: Take exception, sorry?

HELEN: Don't like.

HORVÁTH: Oh. All the same, it's true.

(HELEN *smiles at him.*)

HELEN: You want to go out this evening?

HORVÁTH: No.

HELEN: What do you want to do this evening?

(HORVÁTH *looks at her. Silence.*)

Oh, so that's what you want to do this evening?

HORVÁTH: I think my English is getting better.

(HELEN *gets up and moves away, looking back over her shoulder and smiling seductively. She leaves the room.*
HORVÁTH, *a slow smile spreading in anticipation, rises from the sofa and is about to follow her off, when all of a sudden the house lights snap on, startling him considerably. He moves downstage, peering into the auditorium.*)

39

EIGHT

*Advancing through the auditorium at a leisurely pace, inspecting the
audience suspiciously, chewing a cheap cigar, is a slight, bespectacled
man of forty-three, close-cropped, scruffy and unshaven, a scar on his
left cheek, wearing a flat cap and a jacket with overlong sleeves and
no lapels over an open-necked grey flannel shirt:* BERTOLT BRECHT.

HORVÁTH: Brecht always liked people to be aware that they were
in a theatre. I said to him more than once, but Brecht,
what makes you think they think they're anywhere else?
But he had a way of not answering questions he didn't
approve of.
(*By this time* BRECHT *has reached the stage, and the house
lights are off.*)
Didn't you?
(BRECHT *doesn't answer. Instead, as* HORVÁTH *continues to
speak, he approaches the set and inspects it, reaching up and
rattling one of the flats, shaking his head in dismay.*)
We'd met, of course, in Munich in the early twenties, but I
never really got to know him, he always seemed wary of me;
and I knew that although his teeth, unlike the shark's, were
far from pearly-white, they were sharp enough to make it
advisable to keep out of range of his jaws.
(BRECHT *has found an apple in a fruit bowl on the set. He rubs
it perfunctorily on his trousers and sinks his teeth into it. He
takes his cap off and fans himself.*)
He came direct from Vladivostok, ten days before the Nazis
invaded Russia, just as the State Department was about to
devise a really efficient way of keeping refugees out: they
decided that no one who had surviving close relatives in
Germany should be admitted, on the grounds that they
might be susceptible to pressure and let themselves be
blackmailed into becoming Nazi spies. Consequently, he
was one of the last émigrés to arrive.
BRECHT: Exiles.
(*His voice is metallic, slightly high-pitched, harsh.* HORVÁTH
turns to him, surprised.)

HORVÁTH: What?

BRECHT: I don't like the word émigré. It somehow suggests I left of my own free will. I was driven out. I'm an exile.

HORVÁTH: Just as you like.

BRECHT: Look at this thing. Big and red and shiny and seductive and when you bite it tastes like an old sponge. Capitalist apples.

(*He throws the apple away.*)

HORVÁTH: We heard you were in Moscow.

BRECHT: Yes. But Moscow was no good, we couldn't stay in Moscow.

HORVÁTH: Why not?

BRECHT: I couldn't get enough sugar.

HORVÁTH: Did you have trouble getting out?

BRECHT: Money was the only problem. I had the visas, but I couldn't afford the tickets. Weigel, the children, my two associates, there were six of us, you see. In the end, I had to go to Feuchtwanger's publisher.

HORVÁTH: He gave you money?

BRECHT: Well, I said I was Feuchtwanger's representative authorized by him to collect his royalties. Then I waved a letter from Feuchtwanger in his face. 'How much would you like?' he said. 'How much have you got?' I said.

HORVÁTH: And that was that?

BRECHT: Certainly. Feuchtwanger's very popular in Russia.

HORVÁTH: Did he mind?

BRECHT: No, why should he, he was delighted.

HORVÁTH: There was enough for all of you to get out?

BRECHT: Yes. We had to leave my . . . Grete Steffin, she was ill, she had to go into hospital, she died.

(*Silence.*)

You still do all your writing in bars?

HORVÁTH: I'm not choosy.

BRECHT: I heard that in Vienna you were always to be found in a café otherwise frequented entirely by dwarfs.

HORVÁTH: Yes.

BRECHT: You particularly interested in dwarfs or was it just affectation?

HORVÁTH: Well, you know something, I went to that place for years and in all that time I never met a Nazi midget.

(BRECHT *smiles. Then he plucks at his jacket.*)

BRECHT: It's so hot here, I can't stand this heat, you haven't any ice-cream, have you?

HORVÁTH: Sorry.

BRECHT: You should move out to Santa Monica, it's much cooler.

HORVÁTH: You're not on Argyle any more?

BRECHT: No, Twenty-fifth Street.

HORVÁTH: That's a more appropriate address for you somehow.

BRECHT: The ice-cream is the only thing here I like.

HORVÁTH: You used to be so enthusiastic about America, all those plays you wrote.

BRECHT: That was before I came here.

HORVÁTH: Doesn't say much for the revolution.

(BRECHT *grunts, unsmiling.*)

BRECHT: I wanted to ask you what it was like, working at the studio.

HORVÁTH: Boring. Time-consuming. Pointless.

BRECHT: I've heard it's better to work as a freelance and sell them stories.

HORVÁTH: If they'll buy them, yes, it is better.

BRECHT: Everything here is sell, sell, sell. At home, it's blood and soil and racial purity, here it's sell. If they could, they'd sell their piss to the urinal.

HORVÁTH: You got a car?

BRECHT: No.

HORVÁTH: Then it's no good working at the studio. Not coming in all the way from Santa Monica.

BRECHT: That's what I thought.

HORVÁTH: I'll make some enquiries if you like.

BRECHT: No. I'll manage. I've always despised anyone whose brains can't fill his belly.

(*Silence.*)

HORVÁTH: Seen many people?

BRECHT: Well, I ran into Thomas Mann.

HORVÁTH: How was that?

BRECHT: Like stubbing your toe on three thousand years of history.

(*Silence.*)

I've never felt so remote from the world, not even when I was stuck away in the back end of Finland.

HORVÁTH: You really hate it.

BRECHT: I can't believe there is such a place and I don't know what the hell I'm doing here. I used to read Shelley sometimes and think the poor bastard's been dead a hundred years and all those injustices are still as bad, if not worse, and then I'd think, will they be reading us in another hundred years and feeling the same, and then I'd get depressed for a while. But here I feel like that all the time.

(*Pause.*)

Do you have any Lenin?

HORVÁTH: Lenin?

BRECHT: I didn't want any trouble with customs so I dropped mine over the side at San Pedro.

HORVÁTH: The complete works of Lenin?

BRECHT: Yes.

HORVÁTH: At the bottom of the Los Angeles Harbor?

(*He smiles.* BRECHT *is beginning to look annoyed.*)

No, I don't have any Lenin.

BRECHT: I was afraid of that.

(*He strides off through the auditorium.*)

NINE

HORVÁTH *walks into the set to join* HEINRICH MANN, *turning* en route *to speak over his shoulder to the audience.*

HORVÁTH: One autumn afternoon, Heinrich Mann and I came home early from the studio.

(*Silence.* HEINRICH *shakes his head.*)

HEINRICH: Now what?

HORVÁTH: Something'll turn up. Don't worry.

HEINRICH: I don't know, at my age. . . . What a profession it is. Not only is there no pension, but you're lucky if you get away before they kick your head in.

HORVÁTH: Wish there was something else I could do, but it's too late now, it's all I'm good for. It seems I was born to be a writer.

(*Outside there's a sudden screech of brakes and a muffled thud.*)

HEINRICH: That'll be Nelly.

HORVÁTH: Would you like me to get you something? Just tell me where to find it.

HEINRICH: No, no, it's all right.

(*A moment passes and then* NELLY *enters, holding a glass of red wine. She's very surprised to see them.*)

NELLY: You're back early.

HORVÁTH: Didn't seem much point sitting out the last few hours.

NELLY: No change, eh?

HEINRICH: No.

NELLY: That bloody brother of yours.

HEINRICH: Tommy went personally to see Jack Warner . . .

NELLY: Oh, yeah, squeezed it in, did he, between trips to the White House?

HEINRICH: Nelly, he told me he pleaded with Jack Warner, it can't have been easy.

NELLY: And what happened?

HEINRICH: He says Jack Warner laughed in his face.

(NELLY *pushes her wine abruptly at* HORVÁTH.)

NELLY: Here.

HORVÁTH: Erm . . .

NELLY: Take it. We're not paupers, you know. Yet.

(HORVÁTH *takes the wine and* NELLY *leaves the room briskly.*)

HEINRICH: Strange thought, it's nearly fifty years since my first novel was published. Who could have imagined I'd end up being fired by Jack Warner?

HORVÁTH: We haven't been fired. It's just they're not renewing any of the European Film Fund contracts. It's an important distinction.

(*As he speaks,* NELLY *returns with a full glass, carrying the bottle in her other hand.*)

NELLY: What, you mean like between eating earth and swallowing air?

HORVÁTH: Sort of.

NELLY: So, what are we going to do?

HEINRICH: Well, move to a smaller house, I suppose.

NELLY: We already moved to a smaller house.

HEINRICH: Even smaller.

NELLY: Jesus.

HEINRICH: And I'm afraid the car will have to go.

NELLY: Oh, no.

HEINRICH: Nelly . . .

NELLY: I can't be in this shithole without a car. Why d'you think I went to the trouble and expense of learning how to drive?

HEINRICH: There just isn't any choice.

NELLY: (*To* HORVÁTH) You know what, you know what he did this summer? They wanted to publish a book of his, American publisher, good money. They just asked him to make a few changes, that's all, one or two things they didn't like. So what does he do? He tells them to piss off. (HEINRICH *lowers his head, very unhappy, and shakes it slowly from side to side.*)

HEINRICH: (*Quietly*) I haven't worked all this time to make compromises.

(NELLY *looks at him: her expression softens.*)

NELLY: No, course you haven't, Heini, you're right, you're right, who the hell do these people think they are? (HEINRICH *looks up at her gratefully. She's smiling at him. They look at each other for a moment, then she turns away.*) Well, I can see how this story's going to end.

(*Pause.*)

Back to work is what.

(*She turns to* HORVÁTH.)

Did you know, when Heini met me, I was a barmaid.

HORVÁTH: I had heard.

NELLY: Oh, you had heard, had you, had you heard?

HORVÁTH: Yes.

45

(*She looks at him fiercely for a moment, then relents, pours herself another glass of wine and flops down on the sofa.*)

NELLY: Quite soon after we met, Heini said to me, tell me about your life, I want to know your life story. I'll do one better than that, I said, I'll write it out for you. So I did. So he reads it and he says, this is wonderful, I think I can do something with this. And I says, yeah, I reckon I can do something with it an' all, I can have it published and make a fortune. That's as may be, he says, but listen, just leave it with me for a while. Well, he had it for months. I'd almost forgotten I'd writ the bloody thing. Then one day he says, you know that manuscript you gave me, he says, I've turned it into a novel. Fine, I says, you publish your novel and I'll publish me memoirs, and I'll give you three to one I sell more copies. Yes, he says, that's what I was afraid of, so I took the liberty of dropping your manuscript in the stove.

So don't talk to me about writers.

HORVÁTH: I wouldn't dream of it.

HEINRICH: It was very lively, Nelly's manuscript, but it was a little coarse-grained.

NELLY: That's why it would have been a bestseller, you silly old bugger, then we wouldn't be in this dump.

HORVÁTH: You mean to tell me that's a true story?

HEINRICH: I never contradict a lady.

NELLY: Never do what to a lady, don't you believe it.

(*She chuckles, gets up and crosses to* HORVÁTH, *pours him another drink.*)

Listen, I hear a rumour you've taken up with some Jew.

HEINRICH: Nelly.

NELLY: What's the matter, aren't we good enough for you?

HORVÁTH: I don't know what you mean.

NELLY: Still, I suppose down there at the studio, that's all you could find.

HEINRICH: Nelly!

NELLY: Oh dear, spoken out of turn again.

HORVÁTH: I'm very pleased with the way things have turned out, thank you.

NELLY: Well, that's all that counts.
(*She moves easily back towards the sofa, pouring herself another drink en route. She sits down, smiling pleasantly.*)
So, Ödön, what are you going to do?

HORVÁTH: Well, I'm going to see Siodmak at Universal. He might have something, he's getting on quite well there.
(*Pause.*)
So, if you need some help, I'd be delighted, you know, a loan or whatever.

HEINRICH: My dear boy, it's very kind of you, we do appreciate it. But we shall manage.

HORVÁTH: Well, please don't hesitate. . . .
(*Silence.*)

NELLY: Tell you what, broke or not, we're giving you that fortieth birthday party. Here.

HORVÁTH: Well, I . . .

NELLY: I don't want any of that. I want: thank you, Nelly, how kind.

HORVÁTH: Thank you, Nelly.

NELLY: And just to show all is forgiven, you can even bring your Yid.

HORVÁTH: I don't know if she'll come, she's a bit particular about mixing with Germans.
(NELLY *looks at him for a moment, then grins suddenly.* HORVÁTH *raises his glass.*)
Here's to being unemployed.

TEN

As the toast is drunk and the lights fade, BRECHT *enters, drawing a half-curtain in front of the set, still puffing on a cigar and wearing his hat. He carries a square of green linen, which he arranges carefully on the forestage. When this is laid to his satisfaction, he produces, as if by magic, from inside his jacket, a small sign, which he sets up behind the square. It says:* brecht's garden.
While this has been going on, HORVÁTH *has put down his glass of wine*

47

and moved downstage.

HORVÁTH: As winter drew in and the temperature fell to seventy, I received a postcard from Brecht. It was far from easy to decipher, since Brecht, somewhat literal-mindedly in my view, included punctuation in his crusade against capitalism, as if there were something imperialist about the very concept of a capital b. Anyway, the gist of it was that I was summoned to an audience in Santa Monica.

(*He goes over to join* BRECHT, *who, in the meantime, has sat down on his garden.*)

BRECHT: How are you managing?

HORVÁTH: Carefully. I'm getting eighteen dollars fifty a week unemployment pay.

BRECHT: Wonders of the welfare state.

(HORVÁTH *sits down on the ground, nodding wryly.*)

I thought you might like to write a film with me.

HORVÁTH: Oh?

BRECHT: I'm working on three or four at the moment. With different people. With two of you, you can bang one out in a week. My theory is, if you bombard the studios with stories, they're bound to accept one sooner or later.

HORVÁTH: What sort of stories?

BRECHT: Give you an example, I'm working on one with Thören, do you know him?

HORVÁTH: No.

BRECHT: He's very successful, works for MGM.

HORVÁTH: A girl I know, American, asked me the other day what 'Ars Gratia Artis' meant over the gates at MGM. I told her it meant 'abandon hope all ye who enter here'.

BRECHT: Well, you're right, Thören is impossible. He's all over the place. He keeps saying: Now as I see it, there are three possibilities—he can ask for money *or* he can sacrifice his life for the cause *or* he can make his mother pregnant. It's like working with a chicken with no head. On the other hand, he makes a fortune.

HORVÁTH: And what's the story?

BRECHT: It's a romantic comedy. American and a Portuguese are

48

planning a huge business deal, which they must keep secret
from the competition, so they write to each other in code, in
the form of passionate love letters. American censor, girl,
reads the letters, gets fascinated. Then she meets the man,
who falls for her and pursues her, without knowing she
knows he keeps writing those letters. Endless complications.
Happy ending. It's a piece of shit. Ingrid Bergman would
be great.

HORVÁTH: Why?

BRECHT: Because she's wonderful.

HORVÁTH: What are you calling it?

BRECHT: *Bermuda Troubles*.

(*Silence.*)

What I mean is, it should be possible for you and me to put
our heads together, scientifically, and come up with
something just as good as these mindless hacks.

HORVÁTH: Yes, in theory. Just as bad, you mean.

BRECHT: Doesn't have to be bad. I'm doing a better one for
Charles Boyer. With Kortner.

HORVÁTH: Oh, how's he?

BRECHT: Vitriolic as ever. I like working with him. I made him
angry yesterday. He's been doing the research and he found
out that in the nineteenth century, in the Mediterranean sea
ports, the whores would sometimes have to take on more
than a hundred customers a day. He was very shocked.
Finally I said, 'You bloody liberals are all the same: "A
hundred a day! What inhumanity! Eighty at the most!"'

HORVÁTH: (*Smiling*) He's a good actor.

BRECHT: Very. But there's no work for him here.

HORVÁTH: Why not? Peter Lorre works all the time.

BRECHT: Yes, sinking slowly into the quicksand, grinning from
ear to ear.

(*Silence.*)

HORVÁTH: Whatever happened to Carola Neher?

BRECHT: Neher?

HORVÁTH: Didn't she go to Moscow?

BRECHT: Yes, with her husband, yes.

HORVÁTH: I adored her.

49

BRECHT: Did you?

HORVÁTH: Rumour was, she was your mistress, when she was in
    The Threepenny Opera.

BRECHT: Was it?

HORVÁTH: Did you see her when you were in Moscow?

BRECHT: She was arrested a couple of years ago. They both were.

HORVÁTH: What for?

BRECHT: Ostensibly for Trotskyite activities in Prague.

HORVÁTH: That's ridiculous.

BRECHT: She was always very naive.

HORVÁTH: And what's happened to her?
    (*Silence.* BRECHT *shakes his head.*)

BRECHT: Far as I know, she's dead.

HORVÁTH: How appalling.

BRECHT: The innocent, you know.
    (*Pause.*)
    I think they deserve everything they get.
    (*Long silence. Then* HORVÁTH *rises and moves downstage. As he
    speaks,* BRECHT *picks up his garden and sign and starts to
    move off.* HORVÁTH *touches* BRECHT's *arm and indicates the
    half-curtain, as if to indicate it's no good to him.* BRECHT
    shakes his head pityingly and removes the curtain, revealing
    HEINRICH MANN's *sitting-room.* BRECHT *exits.*)

HORVÁTH: It was good of him to ask me to collaborate with him.
    It was his way of expressing concern. But even as I agreed
    to think it over, I knew we would never be able to work
    together.

ELEVEN

Spot on HORVÁTH.

HORVÁTH: The following weekend the Japanese attacked Pearl
    Harbor. We show folk knew where our duty lay and we
    were not slow to retaliate: all performances of *Madame
    Butterfly* at the Met. were cancelled and Greenwich Village

Savoyards withdrew *The Mikado* from their repertoire. All the Japanese gardeners in Hollywood were fired. In the case of an air raid, *Variety* advised its readers to seek shelter in the Nora Bayes Theater, on the grounds that it had never had a hit.

So: on Sunday, Pearl Harbor. Monday, war was declared. And on Tuesday, I was forty. I've known better starts to the week.

(*Lights up on* HEINRICH MANN'*s sitting-room.* NELLY, *festively dressed, enters with a tray of glasses and an open bottle of wine. She puts the tray down, looks around, quickly pours herself a glass, drinks, and replaces the glass. Then, as* HORVÁTH *continues to speak, the room gradually fills with the personnel from* SALKA VIERTEL'*s party, with the addition of* BRECHT *and* HELENE WEIGEL, *his gaunt, hollow-cheeked wife. Meanwhile,* NELLY *whispers something to* HEINRICH, *and makes her way out to the kitchen.*)

I phoned Nelly to ask her if the party was still on. 'Why shouldn't it be?' she said. It was nine o'clock in the morning. She was drunk.

Helen came by to collect me and drive me over. She was a little late, perhaps because she was nervous about meeting all those formidable Germans.

(HELEN SCHWARTZ *joins him as he comes to the end of his observations, and together they join the fringes of a group being addressed by* THOMAS MANN.)

THOMAS: I'm simply unable to understand what it is they do to their writers here. It happens time and again. They write one good book, then two mediocre ones and that's the end of their career. They have no conception of a developing life-work. No stamina. They get drowned in success.

HELEN: (*To* HORVÁTH) What's he saying?

HORVÁTH: (*In English*) He says there are no American writers.

HELEN: Oh? What about Fitzgerald, Hemingway, Faulkner, Dos Passos, Steinbeck, Nathanael West?

THOMAS: (*In English*) I did not mean to wound your sensibilities, Miss Schwartz. I can only speak as my old-fashioned eyes discover.

(HEINRICH *hands* HORVÁTH *a glass of wine.*)

HORVÁTH: Where's Nelly?

HEINRICH: In the kitchen, I believe, preparing something for you.

HORVÁTH: Shall I go and . . .?

HEINRICH: No, no, I think she wants to surprise you.

BRECHT: (*To* THOMAS) I can't agree with you either. If you want a writer with real inventiveness and staying power, what about Erle Stanley Gardner?

THOMAS: I'm afraid I am not familiar with his work.

BRECHT: Well, he's not Simenon, of course, but he's about the best they have over here.

THOMAS: I'm obliged for the advice.

(*He turns away and* BRECHT *moves off with* WEIGEL, *muttering to her.*)

BRECHT: I can't understand what he's saying half the time, his mouth is full of money.

HEINRICH: Well, the English seem to have got off to a pretty poor start in Libya. After all that build-up.

WEIGEL: What's the world coming to, when Churchill is our only hope?

BRECHT: It doesn't matter how modern their weapons are, I'd say in the hands of the oldest and most corrupt aristocracy in the world, they are bound to misfire.

HORVÁTH: Oh, really, I thought shooting was the one thing the English aristocracy was good at.

HEINRICH: They don't have the spirit of the Russians. Did you see that thing about the fighting in Rostov? They're attacking the Panzer troops with frying pans.

BRECHT: The Nazis have condemned them for illegal methods.

HEINRICH: That's right, tanks are allowed but frying pans are illegal.

BRECHT: All this stuff about the Japanese is all over the front pages, but I found something inside the *LA Times* yesterday I think is much more significant. The German advance on Moscow has broken down because of sub-zero temperatures. So, on the day the greatest industrial power in the world enters the war, it's finally dawned on Hitler that in Russia the winters are cold. He's finished. The house-painter is finished.

HORVÁTH: The Americans will declare war on Germany as well, won't they?

THOMAS: Oh, yes, before the end of the week, I think I can guarantee that.

(*Suddenly, the assembled company is silenced by a raucous sound from the kitchen:* NELLY'*s voice yelling out:* 'Happy Birthday to you . . .' *Everyone turns to look at the kitchen door.* NELLY *appears. Sensation. She's carrying a birthday cake, the candles lit. She's naked.*)

NELLY: (*Singing*) . . . Happy Birthday to you, Happy Birthday dear Ödön, Happy Birthday to you.

(*She hands him the cake, which he takes uncertainly from her. Silence.*)

Well, blow out the candles, aren't you going to blow out the candles?

(HORVÁTH *does so, as best he can.*)

Now you have to make a wish. (*Coquettishly*) Can you think of a wish?

(*Silence.* NELLY *turns away from* HORVÁTH *to include everyone.*)

Well, I've had to sell all my jewellery, every last piece, so I thought, what the hell, why wear anything?

(*She turns on* THOMAS.)

Hello, maestro, you've never seen your sister-in-law like this, have you? Now what do you think of me?

THOMAS: Control yourself.

NELLY: That's all you can say, isn't it? That's all you can think.

HEINRICH: (*Gently*) Nelly.

(*She turns and stares at* HEINRICH *for a few seconds. Then she turns back to* HORVÁTH.)

NELLY: If you knew what it's like to be married to such an old, old man. He's so old. He's so old.

(*She bursts into tears.* HORVÁTH *slips off his jacket and wraps her in it. Then he leads her slowly offstage. Nobody moves. Tableau. Then* HORVÁTH *reappears, in his shirtsleeves, and passes through the guests, taking no notice of them. As he speaks, the lights go down on them and they silently disperse.*)

HORVÁTH: It's true to say that none of us was really happy. But

53

as I expect you've noticed by now, I saw things differently from the others. You see, I had always loved what was strange and half-finished. I loved gullibility, cheap religious mementoes, plastic, superstitions, pornography with spelling mistakes, girls dressed as mermaids, streets without end, the ethics of the fairground, the bright smiles of the no-hopers, motiveless friendliness, the pleasures of nomads'-land. In short, after two years in Los Angeles, I knew I was home. (*He strolls offstage as the house lights come up.*)

ACT TWO

1942–50

TWELVE

Light-show: garish neon. Franz Waxman's music for
Sunset Boulevard. Projections: Hollywood landmarks of the forties.
HORVÁTH *steps into this, grinning.*

HORVÁTH: Ah, Hollywood! The kitsch! The *désespoir*!
  (*He watches the projections for a moment.*)
  The pagodas! The *châteaux*! The mauve haciendas!
  Donuts! Dentistry! Divorce!
  (*Everything snaps off. Total darkness.*)
  The blackout.
  (*Pause.*)
  Right, that's quite enough of that.
  (*Lights up on a corner of the 'Sleeping Beauty', a dingy bar*
  on Hollywood Boulevard. There's a table for one covered with
  papers: among them a glass of red wine. Not far off is another
  table where ANGEL *sits, nursing a scotch on the rocks.* HORVÁTH
  glances at all this, then turns back to the audience.)
  Well, I got by. Siodmak did what he could and before too
  long I had my first credit, shared with only four others, for
  a really sleazy horrorpic, not to be confused with Garbo's
  latest, called *Two-Headed Woman*. In Germany, I'd
  always used a pseudonym for my film work, but here that
  seemed like an unnecessary vanity. I had said goodbye to
  the theatre. I had no reputation to guard any more. I
  moved smoothly along to the next piece of work, which had
  to do with the adventures of a barber-shop quartet.
    I had my routine now. I had a room with a Murphy bed

55

in an apartment building north of Hollywood Boulevard. I'd stroll down the hill, buy a paper on the corner of Hollywood and Wilcox from a charming dwarf called Angelo, have breakfast in the local drugstore, coffee, juice, toast and one egg over easy, then I'd wander past the Crossroads of the World to Sunset and Highland and take a bus across the hills to Universal City. I appreciated the way that even when you were down and out, the place names did their best to make you feel important.

All I needed now was some little haven conducive to work and contemplation; and before long I discovered the ideal spot.

(*He gestures at the set.*)

The 'Sleeping Beauty' Cocktail Bar on Hollywood Boulevard.

(*He goes and sits down at his table, sips at the wine.*)

I even taught, Hal, the barman, how to make a Glühwein, hot red wine with cinnamon. It's hardly the climate for it, but it did make Hal's wine a little more palatable and every sip was molten nostalgia.

(BRECHT *appears and spends a moment peering irritatedly round the dimly lit bar. Then he gestures up at the lighting box. Immediately the stage is saturated in hard white light.*

HORVÁTH *looks up, blinking crossly.*)

There's no need for all that, you know.

BRECHT: Force of habit.

(HORVÁTH *waves to the lighting box and the lighting returns to normal.*)

HORVÁTH: Welcome to the office. What are you drinking?

BRECHT: I don't know.

HORVÁTH: Glühwein?

BRECHT: Christ, no, what a horrible idea.

(*He draws a chair over to* HORVÁTH's *table and sits.*

HORVÁTH, *meanwhile, calls over his shoulder in English.*)

HORVÁTH: Hal? Glass of iced water for my friend.

(BRECHT *contemplates the table for a moment, his expression severe.*)

BRECHT: How can you work in such chaos?

HORVÁTH: I know where everything is.
BRECHT: I need order.
  (HORVÁTH *nods as if* BRECHT *has stated the obvious.* HAL
  *appears, a huge, jovial figure, clutching a glass of iced water in
  his great hand. He puts it down in front of* BRECHT.)
HAL: Big spender, huh, Ed?
BRECHT: What did he say?
  (HORVÁTH *shrugs, diplomatically feigning incomprehension.
  Then he hands his empty glass to* HAL, *frowning in mock
  disapproval.*)
HAL: More of this shit?
HORVÁTH: If you please.
  (HAL *leaves.* BRECHT *watches him go with distaste.*)
  How's work?
BRECHT: Same as ever. Hollywood roulette. At the moment I'm
  writing a picture for Lorre.
HORVÁTH: What about?
BRECHT: He plays an actor, émigré . . .
HORVÁTH: Emigré?
BRECHT: Yes, in London, completely broke, gets taken up by a
  millionaire banker with a palazzo in Berkeley Square.
HORVÁTH: Yes.
BRECHT: Everything's fine until he falls foul of the butler,
  Sniffkins. . . . Oh, forget it.
  (*Silence.*)
HORVÁTH: Sniffkins?
BRECHT: Well . . .
HORVÁTH: Yes.
  (HAL *arrives with* HORVÁTH's *Glühwein. Then he attends to*
  ANGEL, *at the other table, who's been staring over at* HORVÁTH
  and BRECHT.)
BRECHT: I really hate it here.
  (HORVÁTH *looks around.*)
HORVÁTH: It's not so bad, better than my room.
BRECHT: I don't mean this dump, I mean the whole poxy,
  godforsaken city.
HORVÁTH: Oh, I see.
BRECHT: I don't know what I can do here, I feel like a sausage in

a greenhouse.

HORVÁTH: I'm just beginning to enjoy it.

BRECHT: It's pretty, all right, the ocean, the hills, the lemon groves. But if you look more closely you'll see every one of those damn trees has a price tag on it. That's the way it is everywhere here. What have you got? Let's have a look! Deliver the goods! And everything with a smile, all this . . . depraved cuteness.

HORVÁTH: I don't mind that.

BRECHT: And you know what the worst thing is? When you take your place in the line with all the other whores and pimps and pushers, there's one thing you feel more than anything else, and it's what really makes me ill, and what it is is hope.

HORVÁTH: It's certainly a good deal more common than charity or faith.

BRECHT: Shelley said that Hell must be like London, ha, what did he know?

(*Silence.*)

By the way, I found out what it is they do, all those people at the studios.

HORVÁTH: What?

BRECHT: They all have different jobs, you see. One has to check the consistency, another one the quantity, somebody else makes sure it's brown and someone else again tests it for smell. Finally, they get together, all these specialists, and compare notes. Only then do they let themselves get excited: It is! It really is! It's genuine, cover-to-cover shit! Let's shoot it!

HORVÁTH: And of course, once they shoot it, it's dead.

BRECHT: Yes; and I also found out the secret of being a successful screenwriter.

HORVÁTH: Tell me.

BRECHT: You have to write badly, you have to write very, very badly, *but you also have to write as well as you possibly can.* (*Pause while* HORVÁTH *works this out. Then he smiles broadly.*)

Anyway, what the hell's the use of a medium that can't react to its audience?

58

HORVÁTH: All the same, you're still trying.

BRECHT: Unsolved is not the same as insoluble.

HORVÁTH: Well, that didn't come out of a fortune cookie.

BRECHT: It's depressing, though. The other day I was working on some rewrites in a play and something which hardly ever happens: I got stuck. And for the first time, suddenly, I had a glimpse of what it must be like to be untalented. (*Silence.*)

HORVÁTH: Was there something special you wanted to see me about?

BRECHT: Heinrich Mann.

HORVÁTH: What about him?

BRECHT: He's starving to death.

HORVÁTH: Surely not.

BRECHT: Literally.

HORVÁTH: I thought Thomas sent him a cheque every month.

BRECHT: He sends some measly amount. Last month it didn't arrive. So, not only no groceries, but his teeth were hurting and he couldn't go back to the dentist, because he owes him.

HORVÁTH: I gave Nelly some money last time I saw her.

BRECHT: You mustn't do that. She just drinks it.

HORVÁTH: I don't care what she does with it.

BRECHT: Well, it doesn't get to him is what I'm trying to say.

HORVÁTH: All right, I can give you a hundred. But you're going to have to wait till the end of the week.

BRECHT: OK. Thanks. Thanks.

HORVÁTH: I can't believe Thomas is allowing this to happen.

BRECHT: What does he care? He basks up there in the Palisades, like some old lizard, wallowing in money, with his secretary and his servants and his five cars and his brother's down here, sweating and broke, with an insane wife and not even enough to get his shoes repaired. It's like an image of everything that's most depressing about our profession. Heinrich saw the way things were going before the last war, he understood about Fascism, while Hitler was still slapping paint on beer halls. Thomas thought that war was just what Dr Nietzsche ordered, he supported it, he thought

59

democracy was some new-fangled French fad that wouldn't last ten minutes in Germany.

HORVÁTH: But he changed his mind.

BRECHT: That's exactly what I mean. Any opinion he holds today is an opinion he opposed five years ago. He's been rewarded for having been as slow-witted and impotent as his bourgeois public. And Heinrich's been punished because he was right all along.

HORVÁTH: Literature has to do with more than being right.

BRECHT: Literature? His books can be of no benefit to anyone. Except possibly weightlifters. But that's not what I'm talking about. Did you know Hitler was in power three years before Thomas Mann could bring himself to say a word against him? That's what I'm talking about.

HORVÁTH: I can't condemn him for that.

BRECHT: Well, I can. And I do. And you should.

(*Silence.*)

HORVÁTH: I'll give you the money on Saturday. Anonymously, if you don't mind.

BRECHT: I don't mind.

(*He looks at his watch.*)

I guess it's time we were going.

HORVÁTH: We?

BRECHT: The curfew.

HORVÁTH: Oh.

BRECHT: I suppose we're lucky they haven't put us in camps like the Japanese.

HORVÁTH: What's this us?

BRECHT: Us Germans.

HORVÁTH: I'm a Hungarian.

(BRECHT *frowns, puzzled.* HORVÁTH *smiles blandly.* BRECHT *rises to his feet, looking slightly annoyed. He stretches out his hand. Perfunctory handshake.*)

BRECHT: Goodbye.

HORVÁTH: Goodbye.

(BRECHT *leaves. Hiatus.* HORVÁTH *shuffles one or two of his papers idly. Then he looks up and catches the eye of* ANGEL *at the next table. She smiles at him. Brief silence.*)

ANGEL: Mind if I join you?

HORVÁTH: Please.

(*She gets up and crosses to his table.*)

Hal!

(*She sits.* HAL *appears.* HORVÁTH *gestures at her glass.*)

Ordinary red wine this time for me.

HAL: Ordinary's what it is.

(*He goes.* HORVÁTH *smiles at* ANGEL.)

ANGEL: Thought your friend was never going to go.

HORVÁTH: Me too.

(HAL *brings the drinks.*)

What's your name?

ANGEL: Just call me Angel.

HORVÁTH: You're an actress.

ANGEL: How did you know?

(HORVÁTH *smiles.*)

Maybe you've seen me in something.

HORVÁTH: Maybe.

ANGEL: I had a swell scene in *West Point Widow*. But they cut it.

HORVÁTH: Shame.

ANGEL: And I was in *Destry Rides Again*. In all the saloon scenes.

HORVÁTH: And here you are again. Cheers.

(*They drink.*)

ANGEL: He was getting pretty excited, your friend.

HORVÁTH: He does.

ANGEL: I thought maybe you was spies.

HORVÁTH: (*Mock indignation*) Spies? I'm a Hungarian.

ANGEL: Gee.

HORVÁTH: No, I am no spy. But I am an enemy alien. This means I have to be indoors by eight o'clock. Curfew.

ANGEL: Oh.

HORVÁTH: So we will have to continue our discussions at my place.

(*He rises to his feet.* ANGEL *looks up at him, a touch hesitant.*)

ANGEL: You got a car?

HORVÁTH: I only live just up the hill.

ANGEL: What do you do?

HORVÁTH: I work at Universal, same as you.

(*Silence. Then she gets up, smiling, and takes his arm. They stroll out of the bar together, favoured by a sardonic grin from* HAL.)

THIRTEEN

Light change. HAL *is still behind the bar washing glasses. He looks up as* HORVÁTH *strolls in on his own.*

HAL: Hi, Ed.

HORVÁTH: Red wine, I think, tonight.

HAL: No, it's too hot for that. What you want is a nice Chablis.

HORVÁTH: I need your opinion, I send you a postcard.

(HAL *enjoys this. By this time,* HORVÁTH *is at his table, stirring his mess of papers.* HAL *vanishes offstage.* HORVÁTH *concentrates on his papers for a moment. From outside, the screech of brakes. After a time,* NELLY MANN *makes an uncertain entrance, peering around the bar.* HORVÁTH *looks up and sees her before she sees him.*)

Nelly.

(*She blinks at him and smiles unsteadily. He crosses to her and shakes her hand. Then he leads her back to his table.*)

Hal!

HAL: (*Offstage*) Yeah? Now what?

HORVÁTH: Bring the bottle.

(*He helps* NELLY *into a seat.*)

How are you?

NELLY: Fine. I'm fine.

HORVÁTH: And Heinrich?

NELLY: Oh, he's fine.

(HAL *appears with an opened bottle of wine and a glass.*)

HAL: Shall I pour it out or do I leave it to breathe?

HORVÁTH: Go shit in your hat.

HAL: That's good! (*To* NELLY.) He's improving. (*To* HORVÁTH.) I'm proud of you.

(*He goes, glancing at* NELLY, *who hasn't reacted at all.*
HORVÁTH *pours a glass of wine for her. She drinks it off, fast.
He pours her another.*)

HORVÁTH: I heard things had been a bit difficult.

NELLY: Yes. It was sweet of you to give us money.

HORVÁTH: Who told you? I . . .

NELLY: Nobody. I guessed.

(*Silence.*)

HORVÁTH: Brecht said . . .

NELLY: Yes, that was all a bit of an exaggeration. Tommy's
cheque went astray in the post. He was away. Panic. When
he came back he wrote another cheque and paid off all
Heini's debts. He's not a bad old sod. Except him and
Heini's not on speaking terms any more.

HORVÁTH: Why not?

NELLY: Oh, my fault, I suppose.

(*She pours herself another glass of wine, as she is to throughout
the rest of the scene.*)

He came around to read us another great chunk of that
terrible old *Joseph* crap. I was in the kitchen and I was
just singing to myself, you know, to cut out the drone,
when he suddenly says very loud: Is that the dog? Is that
the dog, I ask you? We haven't got a bloody dog. So I says:
No, it's me. And he shouts in: I know you've never had a
very high opinion of my work. . . . I don't know, I said,
anyone who can write the line: 'Like all the Krögers, she
looked distinguished' has to have some talent.

HORVÁTH: I don't understand.

NELLY: Kröger, it's me maiden name. Nelly Kröger. Fine old
German name.

HORVÁTH: Oh, I see.

NELLY: Anyway, he perks up a bit and says: I never knew you
were an admirer of *Buddenbrooks*. I don't know about
admirer, I said, but the first four pages were ever so good.
(*Silence. She drinks.*)

It's not him, really, he's all right; it's his wife. Jewish cow.

HORVÁTH: Nelly, do stop.

NELLY: You know what he said to Heini, when he came back

63

from his first date with her? He said: You know, she's not a
bit like a Jew.

HORVÁTH: Really?

NELLY: Shows how much he knew. I don't know, there's him
and there's you and there's Brecht, what's so special about
them?

HORVÁTH: I don't want to talk about it, Nelly.

NELLY: Where's yours, then?

HORVÁTH: In New York.

NELLY: Oh, and when the cat's away?

HORVÁTH: We try not to think in those terms.

NELLY: You know what, you can be a real pompous bastard
when you put your mind to it.

(HORVÁTH *looks hurt*.)

Come on, cheer up.

(*Silence.*)

HORVÁTH: So you're all right for money now?

NELLY: Yes. Tommy does what he can for us. He's not as rich
as everybody thinks he is. Heini told him to keep the Nobel
Prize money in Switzerland, lots of people did, but he
wouldn't listen and the Nazis took the lot. They stole his
house and the SA Commandant in Munich is driving his
car.

(*Pause.*)

I got a job, what about that, then? In a hospital.

HORVÁTH: Nursing?

NELLY: Washing sheets.

(*Silence. She drinks.*)

Yes, that's right, it's awful. But at least I've been able to
buy a car. On credit.

HORVÁTH: Is it worth it?

NELLY: Course it is. Also I did something clever. Really dozy
bitch handling the sale, so I gave my name as Kröger. That
way if there's any problems with the car, I can just sell it
and get another one.

HORVÁTH: You can't be serious.

NELLY: Why not? They'd never find me. I even gave them a
false address. Brecht's.

(*She chuckles.* HORVÁTH *shakes his head wonderingly.*)

HORVÁTH: You'll get in terrible trouble.

NELLY: I been in trouble all me life. That's one of the reasons I hate this place, it's so boring.

(HORVÁTH *looks at his watch.*)

HORVÁTH: I'm sorry to say this, Nelly, but I think it's time we were going. The curfew . . .

NELLY: There's no curfew for you. You're a bleeding Hungarian.

HORVÁTH: I know, but there is for you.

NELLY: Well, why don't you let me worry about that?

HORVÁTH: Let me take you home.

NELLY: I didn't know you could drive.

HORVÁTH: Anyone can drive.

(*Silence.*)

NELLY: I could always spend the night at your place.

(*She stares boldly across the table at him.* HORVÁTH *looks back at her, confused but tempted.*)

HORVÁTH: That's right, you could.

(*He breaks off, reflects for a moment.*)

What about Heinrich?

NELLY: He doesn't mind.

HORVÁTH: Of course he minds.

NELLY: Listen, how would you know, he's not your bloody husband, you don't have to live with him.

HORVÁTH: I have to live with myself.

NELLY: I don't need all these bloody excuses, if you don't fancy it, just say.

HORVÁTH: It really isn't that at all.

(*Silence.*)

NELLY: I'm so lonely.

(*Pause.*)

Do you want me to say please?

(*Pause.*)

Please.

(HORVÁTH *sits there, torn.* NELLY *puts a hand over her eyes and starts sobbing silently.* HORVÁTH *reaches over to touch her arm.*)

HORVÁTH: I'll take you home.
   (*She pulls away from him.*)
NELLY: I'm not going anywhere near that squalid dump tonight.
HORVÁTH: Well, then, I'll take you wherever you want to go.
NELLY: I'll take myself.
   (*She's on her feet, takes two steps away from the table, then turns back, grabs the wine bottle, turns away again and hurries out.* HORVÁTH *watches her go, then sits for a moment, pondering. Then he looks up at the audience.*)
HORVÁTH: I didn't normally allow conscience or sentiment to influence me in these matters. Indeed, I lost my virginity in Budapest with a nice married woman whose husband was away at the front. It was just the image of that old man sitting alone in that tiny house on South Swall Drive, waiting.

FOURTEEN

Clear winter day. HORVÁTH *and* HELEN *stroll along a deserted beach, arm-in-arm. Roar of the surf.*

HELEN: When I was back East, somebody gave me some transcripts of the speeches Thomas Mann's been making for the BBC.
HORVÁTH: Yes.
HELEN: He says they've been taking Jews out of Holland and sending them to be gassed.
HORVÁTH: Yes, this is easily possible.
HELEN: But if they're doing that, what can they be doing to the Jews *in* Germany?
   (HORVÁTH *hesitates before answering.*)
HORVÁTH: I don't know, but if you imagine the worst you can imagine, probably it will be worse.
HELEN: But what's happening? I'm a member of the Anti-Nazi League, but nobody's told us about these things. Why
66

don't we know more about it? Why doesn't somebody do
something?

HORVÁTH: What can anyone do?

HELEN: I think just standing by and letting it happen is as bad as
taking part in it.

HORVÁTH: Well . . .

(*He looks away. She stops, releases his arm and stands still,
looking at him. He comes to a ragged halt, still avoiding her
eye.*)

HELEN: Don't you care about it?

HORVÁTH: Of course I care about it. From the beginning I have
been writing about how Germany is. Perhaps I am not
enough a good writer. In any case, no one has listened.
What can I say about history? People like to watch
accidents.

HELEN: Sometimes I think you're very cold.

HORVÁTH: Yes. Well, yes.

(*Silence.*)

HELEN: Well, I need at least to feel I'm trying to do something,
even if it's an illusion. I've decided to join the Party.

HORVÁTH: The Communist Party?

HELEN: Yes.

(HORVÁTH *shrugs, his expression dubious.*)
You disapprove?

HORVÁTH: I can't take these people seriously. Here in America,
the far Left, compared to the Left in Europe, they're like
Republicans. Every other kind of extremism you have, but
you don't seem to have the talent for political extremism.

HELEN: I'm not interested in extremism, I'm interested in
getting things done: opening the Second Front, repealing
the Smith Act, helping to organize the migrant workers.

HORVÁTH: All this is fine. I just don't like to join.

HELEN: No commitments, uh?

HORVÁTH: Yes, maybe.

HELEN: Feel the same about politics as you do about people?

HORVÁTH: I like to keep . . . freedom of action, yes. Also, I have
very bad experiences with joinings. All kinds.

HELEN: So you've given up. Too old, right?

67

HORVÁTH: I think a writer must be always outside. You tell better the truth from standing looking in the window than from sitting at the table.

HELEN: Yes, but why should you have to stand on your own?

(HORVÁTH *hesitates a moment before deciding to confront the question.*)

HORVÁTH: Why do you ask me these questions? You know how important is maintaining independence. For your work also.

HELEN: I know, but with you there's no choice.

HORVÁTH: If this was wrong for you, we would not still be friends after years.

HELEN: I wasn't talking about us anyway. I was talking about taking a stand.

HORVÁTH: Is the same thing, you see. In America, everything is personal. So if I smile at the Communist Party, it is because for me is like a game, a luxury you can afford if you have too much compassion in the bank. In Europe is life or death.

HELEN: That doesn't entitle you to be patronizing.

HORVÁTH: I know this, and I don't mean it, but I also know what you have to do in Europe just to get through the day. And I left in 'thirty-eight, before the real horrors started. Even so, there are things in my conscience you would never believe.

HELEN: I expect I might be able to guess.

HORVÁTH: No. Never.

(*He stands for a moment, looking out to sea.*)

HELEN: Soon be warm enough to swim.

HORVÁTH: Not for me, not here. This goddam sea is too big. I need a human scale and a flat water.

HELEN: Why is it, when it comes to anything really large, you're afraid to let yourself go?

(*Silence. Instead of answering,* HORVÁTH *begins to stroll along the beach again.* HELEN *lets him go a few paces, then follows.*)

HORVÁTH: You know what, I am starting to write a play.

HELEN: Really?

(*She catches up with him, pleased, and takes his arm.*)

HORVÁTH: That's right. First time in five years.

HELEN: But that's wonderful.
    (HORVÁTH *gives a wry grimace.*)
    Isn't it?
HORVÁTH: I don't know. It hurts. Like learning to walk on a broken leg. But it will give me something to do evenings when you are at the, you know, meetings.
    (HELEN *almost bridles, then decides not to take offence. They stroll off, arm-in-arm.*)

FIFTEEN

Music: orchestral version of Friedrich Holländer's 'Und Sonst Gar Nichts' ('Falling in Love Again') from The Blue Angel. *Lights up on* HEINRICH MANN, *sitting alone, as imagined by* HORVÁTH, *in his small sitting-room, staring at the wall.*
Doorbell. HEINRICH *doesn't stir. Doorbell again. This time he registers it and slowly rises to his feet. The music fades as he crosses to the door and lets* HORVÁTH *in. They shake hands, and* HEINRICH *gives a small formal bow. Forming the background to this scene, occasional sounds of passing traffic.* HEINRICH *shows* HORVÁTH *to the chair he has been sitting in.*

HEINRICH: It's very good of you to come so promptly.
HORVÁTH: It's a pleasure.
HEINRICH: I know what it is, getting about in this town.
HORVÁTH: What can I do for you?
HEINRICH: It's Nelly.
HORVÁTH: Oh?
HEINRICH: I'm very worried about her. And I know she thinks a great deal of you, so I was hoping you might be able to . . . help her.
HORVÁTH: In what way?
HEINRICH: I may as well come to the point. She seems to have got herself into trouble. She ran into a parked car and she was arrested. Thank God, for some reason, they failed to notice she was drunk, but she's on some kind of reckless

69

driving charge and there's also, I mean I don't understand the ins and outs of it, this is the second car she's had just recently, and there seems to be some kind of irregularity in the paperwork. She's always been very careless about that kind of thing, and what with the language difficulties. . . . Anyway, she's in despair about it. She's convinced they'll send her to prison.

(*Pause.*)

I just thought maybe you could help to reassure her. Make her see sense.

HORVÁTH: Well, I'll do whatever I can . . . where is she?

HEINRICH: I don't know. She said she was going to work, but I'm sure she hasn't been in all week.

HORVÁTH: Well, suppose I start by finding a pay phone and calling the hospital?

HEINRICH: That's very sensible, but I've already done that myself.

HORVÁTH: I see.

HEINRICH: I thought perhaps you might have some idea of where she might spend her time. I don't really know, you see, how well you know her.

HORVÁTH: Well, I, well, no.

(*The doorbell rings.* HEINRICH *looks up, surprised, and goes across to open the door. After a few murmured words, he lets in a saturnine, fortyish figure:* JACOB LOMAKHIN, *the Soviet consul from San Francisco. He speaks with a heavy Russian accent.* HEINRICH *leads him into the room.*)

HEINRICH: Ödön, Ödön von Horváth, this is Jacob . . .

LOMAKHIN: Jacob Mironovich Lomakhin, at your service.

HEINRICH: Herr Lomakhin is down on a visit from San Francisco. What can I get for you? No vodka, I'm afraid, but I think there may be some wine in the house.

LOMAKHIN: No, no thank you, Herr Mann, in fact, perhaps I call back later, my business is rather confidential.

HEINRICH: Herr von Horváth is a respected colleague. I have no secrets from him. (*To* HORVÁTH) Herr Lomakhin is the Soviet Consul.

HORVÁTH: Perhaps it's time I was on my way . . .

70

HEINRICH: No, no, I insist.

(*All this has happened very quickly and now there is an awkward silence.*)

LOMAKHIN: Very well.

(*He reaches into his inside pocket, brings out two large bundles of banknotes, and slaps them down on the table.*) On behalf of Soviet government, it gives me greatest pleasure, Herr Mann, to make presentation of some monies against your Russian-language royalties.

HEINRICH: I don't know what to say.

LOMAKHIN: These represent small fraction of what is owing. You see your books have sold more than half million copies in Soviet Union.

HEINRICH: No.

LOMAKHIN: So, as I say, should be more, but I hope you will find these acceptable.

HEINRICH: I'm overwhelmed, when your nation is in the midst of such a bitter struggle, that you should . . .

(*LOMAKHIN holds up a hand, interrupting him.*)

LOMAKHIN: Please, please. Is great honour for me.

(*He turns to HORVÁTH, charming smile.*) Herr von . . .?

HORVÁTH: Horváth.

LOMAKHIN: You are also writer.

HORVÁTH: Plays mostly.

LOMAKHIN: I stand open to correction, but I don't believe your work is performed in Soviet Union.

HORVÁTH: Heigh ho.

LOMAKHIN: Yes.

(*At this moment, there's the sound of a key in the door and NELLY appears. She freezes on the threshold.*)

NELLY: Is this the police?

(*HEINRICH hurries over to her.*)

HEINRICH: No, no, no. This is Ödön and this gentleman is the Soviet Consul. Herr Lomakhin, my wife, Nelly.

(*LOMAKHIN bows deep. NELLY stares at him suspiciously, as HEINRICH closes the door behind her.*)

LOMAKHIN: *Enchanté.*

NELLY: What's he want?

HEINRICH: He's brought us some money. My Russian royalties.

NELLY: What?

(HEINRICH *indicates the money. She stares at it incredulously.*)
My God.

(*She rushes impulsively over to* LOMAKHIN *and kisses him on both cheeks. He takes a step back, startled.*)
That's for Stalingrad.

LOMAKHIN: Thank you.

NELLY: It's a miracle, what you people are doing.

LOMAKHIN: We think, when we break through, it will be turning point of war.

NELLY: God knows last year was the saddest year of my life, and this one's been even worse, but the way you Russians have kept your end up . . . It's been an inspiration to us all.

(HORVÁTH *has been watching her, slightly taken aback by this outburst;* LOMAKHIN, *on the other hand, is delighted.*)

LOMAKHIN: You're very kind. I appreciate.

NELLY: No, no, it's us. We appreciate. Have a drink.

LOMAKHIN: Thank you, Frau Mann, but no. I have some other business to attend to . . .

NELLY: Go on, be a devil.

LOMAKHIN: No, really. I am so pleased. Good afternoon.

HEINRICH: I'll show you to your car.

LOMAKHIN: No, no, thank you. I am usually followed by FBI boys. Today, I think I have given them slip, as we say in America, but to be on safe side, I park two, three blocks away. I would not wish to give you embarrassment. So I say good morning.

(*He shakes hands with them. General salutations. He leaves.*
NELLY *picks up one of the bundles of money.*)

NELLY: How much?

HEINRICH: Later, dear, we have a visitor.

NELLY: Well, so we do. Long time no see, how are you, Ödön, don't answer that, back in a minute.

(*She drops the money and vanishes into the kitchen.*
HORVÁTH *looks at* HEINRICH, *who shakes his head to dissuade* HORVÁTH *from saying anything.* NELLY *returns from the*

kitchen with a glass of red wine.)

So, Heini tell you what's happened?

HORVÁTH: Yes.

NELLY: And aren't you going to say, I told you so?

HORVÁTH: No, I'm not.

NELLY: Then what are you going to say?

HORVÁTH: I don't know, I. . . . Your husband says you're very worried about this whole business.

NELLY: Wouldn't you be?

HORVÁTH: Is there anything . . . I mean, do you have a lawyer?

NELLY: (*Pleasantly*) Listen, why don't you piss off and let us count our money?

HEINRICH: Nelly, really.

HORVÁTH: No, no, she's quite right. I'm afraid I can't be much help.

(*He turns and moves abruptly downstage. Lights fade on* HEINRICH *and* NELLY.)

That night Nelly took an overdose of sleeping pills. She was rushed to hospital and her stomach was pumped. She wasn't fit to appear in court. Heinrich did his best to smooth things over. She was sent for a spell to Camarillo State Hospital.

SIXTEEN

Spot on HORVÁTH.

HORVÁTH: In the New Year, all kinds of things began to improve. First, to begin at the bottom, my career. There was, for a brief moment, a vogue for anti-Nazi films. Brecht, for example, had written one for Fritz Lang. And now Siodmak managed to persuade someone at Universal that my novel, about which we had had our original meeting all those years ago in Paris, would make a good film. So, I was able to move into a two-room apartment, buy a pre-war black Studebaker (fortunately, as my driving methods were individual, a sturdy vehicle), and, most important of all, work on a screenplay with other than a mechanical professionalism.

But all of this, of course, was completely insignificant compared to the tremendous excitement of knowing that the tide had finally turned against Hitler. The prospect of peace, needless to say, immediately unleashed a series of bitter quarrels among the émigrés.

(*Lights up on* SALKA VIERTEL'*s front room, less festively arrayed, of course, than it was for* HEINRICH MANN'*s birthday. Present are* HEINRICH *and* THOMAS MANN, BRECHT, FEUCHTWANGER *and three or four others, all men. Discussion is raging.* HORVÁTH *watches a moment, his expression glum. He goes reluctantly over to join the others.*)

THOMAS: I still think the opening is a shade abrupt. Couldn't we agree on some appropriate preamble? Just to explain who we are.

BRECHT: Anyone who reads the letter will know who we are.

THOMAS: I don't so much mean who we are as what we are.

BRECHT: Isn't the fact of the matter this business about mentioning the Soviet Union?

THOMAS: Certainly, I don't think it's altogether prudent to talk about the Soviet Union in the opening clause of the letter. The Americans won't like it, you know. Do we have to refer to Russia at all?

(BRECHT *sighs audibly.*)

BRECHT: We've already discussed all this *ad nauseam*. How can we respond to an initiative coming out of the Soviet Union without saying that's what we're doing?

THOMAS: I don't want you to get the impression I'm at all hostile to Russia. On the contrary, I made a record to be distributed to the Red Army, congratulating them on their noble victories.

BRECHT: I expect they'd have preferred you singing 'Lili Marlene'.

THOMAS: Shall we return to the matter in hand?

BRECHT: All right, if you want to write another sentence, write another sentence and we'll consider it.

74

(*Silence.*)

HEINRICH: What I don't think much of is this business about 'the Hitler régime and those elements favourable to it'. That's a bit clumsy, isn't it? A bit vague?

BRECHT: 'Classes' would be better than 'elements'.

(THOMAS *looks up sharply from his piece of paper.*)

THOMAS: Oh, really, do you think so?

HEINRICH: Why don't we come right out and say what we mean? The Hitler régime and the *corporations*?

THOMAS: I don't think that would be at all advisable. When the Vice-President introduced my speech at Madison Square Gardens, he made it quite clear that any criticism of . . .

HEINRICH: All right, all right.

THOMAS: We're visitors in this country, Heinrich. It's only polite to be circumspect.

BRECHT: (*Muttering*) God help us.

THOMAS: What about 'the Hitler régime and its criminal supporters'?

HEINRICH: Oh, go on, finish your sentence.

(*Silence.*)

HORVÁTH: Couldn't we fetch the ladies?

BRECHT: Why?

HORVÁTH: They'd be able to wrap this up in ten minutes.

(*Silence. Then* THOMAS *looks up.*)

THOMAS: Now. I don't see how anyone could object to this. (*He reads:*) At a moment when the Allied victory approaches, we, the undersigned German writers . . .

HORVÁTH: German?

BRECHT: Writers?

(*Pause.* THOMAS *frowns.*)

THOMAS: We, the undersigned German-speaking writers, scientists and artists consider it our duty to make the following public statement: how's that?

BRECHT: Wonderful.

THOMAS: Any objections?

(*Silence.*)

I feel that softens the hammer-blow of the opening, don't you?

(*Silence.*)
Well, Horváth, as you're so anxious to fetch the ladies,
please do, and we'll try it out on them.
(HORVÁTH *leaves the room.*)

HEINRICH: You know what I think, Tommy? I think we have
laboured mightily and brought forth a mouse.
(THOMAS *frowns but replies imperturbably.*)

THOMAS: Mice have their uses.
(HORVÁTH *returns with* NELLY *and* KATJA MANN, HELENE
WEIGEL, SALKA VIERTEL *and* MARTA FEUCHTWANGER.
Murmured greetings. THOMAS *clears his throat, stands and
picks up his piece of paper. Silence.*)
At a moment . . .
(*He's interrupted by a hoot of laughter from* NELLY. *He looks
at her, pained. She's pointing at the piece of paper.*)

NELLY: That all you come up with in four hours, Jesus, Mary
and Joseph, call yourselves writers?

THOMAS: Nelly, please.
(*She controls herself with some difficulty. Silence falls.*
THOMAS *clears his throat and starts again.*)
At a moment when the Allied victory approaches . . .
(HORVÁTH *slips away downstage as* THOMAS's *voice fades
away and the lights dim.*)

HORVÁTH: Well, I'd had enough, quite enough, more than
enough, so I took the opportunity, as he read, to melt
away. I was passing through Westwood Village before it
dawned on me that I'd forgotten to sign the letter . . .

SEVENTEEN

Spot on HORVÁTH.

HORVÁTH: I was scarcely out of bed the next morning when
there was an insistent pounding on my front door.
(*Insistent pounding. Lights up on* HORVÁTH's *modest sitting-
room. He crosses it, sighing with some annoyance, to open the*
76

front door. BRECHT *enters. Without saying anything, he advances into the room, unfurling a large banner, which he displays prominently and which stays in place throughout the scene. It says:* TWO FELLOW DRAMATISTS REACH THE PARTING OF THE WAYS. HORVÁTH *considers the banner dubiously for a moment, then turns to look questioningly at* BRECHT.)

BRECHT: You'll never guess what that old reptile's done.

HORVÁTH: What old reptile?

BRECHT: He phoned Feuchtwanger this morning and withdrew his signature.

HORVÁTH: Do you mean Thomas Mann?

BRECHT: You call a meeting because you want to say something like this: Hitler is not the same as Germany and we call on our comrades there to rise up against him. Fine. Except the meeting is dominated by some pernickety old maiden aunt who fiddles about with it for hours until it says: It's our view or at any rate the view of most of us or at least the view of enough of us to make it perhaps worth stating that Hitler is *not necessarily* identical in every respect with the rest of the German people and we think it would be awfully nice if some way could be devised of making this clear to the rest of the world, preferably without giving offence and providing of course we make absolutely sure no Commies are involved. Then he calls up the next morning and says, that letter, oh dear, I think that was pitching it a bit strong, you'd better take my name off it.

HORVÁTH: Did he give any reason?

BRECHT: Apparently Roosevelt has some crazy idea that in a putative post-war capitalist Germany, Thomas Mann would make an ideal President. Of course, he keeps modestly declining, like some simpering geriatric virgin, but the fact of the matter is he doesn't dare offend the State Department. Also he says it's too soon to declare our support for the German people, when we don't know what horrors may be uncovered in the future.

HORVÁTH: That seems to me a fair point.

BRECHT: Oh, really, it seems to me equivocating crap.

HORVÁTH: It's not as straightforward as all that, this business about the German people: after all, they did vote for Hitler in pretty considerable numbers.

BRECHT: Well, you know I don't altogether approve of elections.

HORVÁTH: That's another matter.

BRECHT: No, the only thing that makes me suspicious about the Germans is that for thirty years, and without being compelled to do so by twenty divisions of the SS, so many of them obstinately persisted in reading the works of Thomas Mann.

HORVÁTH: There's nothing wrong with Thomas Mann. Except that he believes his reviews.

BRECHT: And you sneaked off without signing the damn thing at all.

HORVÁTH: Coffee?

BRECHT: Sure.

(HORVÁTH *fetches a coffee pot and cups. He pours coffee as* BRECHT *lights a cigar.* BRECHT *collects the coffee, ladles in quantities of sugar.* HORVÁTH *grimaces.*)

HORVÁTH: How can you smoke those evil things?

BRECHT: These? They're El Capitan Corona. I have them sent from New York.

HORVÁTH: You mean you smoke them by choice?

BRECHT: Oh, yes, for me, these are the means of production.

HORVÁTH: You're doing better now at least, aren't you? I saw your Lang film. Some good things in it.

BRECHT: It was shit. They screwed me.

HORVÁTH: How?

BRECHT: First of all it was misery working with Lang. Misery. Every suggestion I made he said: They won't buy that. That they won't buy. Sometimes he said: Yes, they'll buy that. Finally I said: Listen, I know in this country they keep artists in cells padded with money, but do you have to remind me of that every time you open your mouth? Then they cheated me on the credit. It was my film even though they fucked it up. I took it to arbitration at the Screenwriters' Guild. I worked with that bastard Wexley every day for ten weeks and at the hearing he came on as if

78

we'd hardly even met. You know what, just being in the same room with all those moral cripples, I could taste the vomit at the back of my nostrils. And to top it all off, they underpaid me.

HORVÁTH: But you did make some money?

BRECHT: Yeah. Bought some new trousers.

HORVÁTH: And a Buick.

BRECHT: Yes, with a rumble seat.

(*Silence.*)

What happened to your film with Siodmak?

HORVÁTH: We missed the wave. Apparently they've stopped making anti-Nazi films. So Siodmak's doing *Son of Dracula*.

BRECHT: See what I mean? Not that the theatre's any better here. It's all part of the same great emotions racket.

HORVÁTH: I don't know anyone in the theatre.

BRECHT: The way it works, it's so naked. Somebody gets an idea, Ben Hecht, say, and then he goes round personally to all the investors and explains it to them. And they say: Great, Ben, put me down for a thousand dollars. Can you imagine? If you talk to anyone about a theatre collective, they look at you as if you just escaped from Camarillo.

HORVÁTH: I heard a good definition of a theatre collective the other day: a theatre collective is a group of actors and technicians who, after frank, exhaustive and democratic discussion of any given topic, will then decide to do exactly what Brecht wants.

BRECHT: Oh, yes, who said that?

HORVÁTH: Can't remember.

BRECHT: Well, let's face it, when it comes to directing, there's Chaplin and there's me.

(*Silence.* BRECHT *takes a piece of paper out of his inside pocket.*)

Now. What about this signature?

(*He hands the piece of paper to* HORVÁTH, *who looks at it for a moment.*)

HORVÁTH: I genuinely forgot to sign last night. I just wanted to get out of there. But now I look at it . . . No one's interested in what I think about all this: *I'm* not even interested in what I think about it.

(*He hands the piece of paper back to* BRECHT.)

BRECHT: So you're chickening out as well.

HORVÁTH: No. I just can't see the point of it. It seems meaningless and self-important.

BRECHT: To do nothing is as bad as to be on their side.

HORVÁTH: I know that. And I've done far worse things than not sign this bit of paper. But that's my business, isn't it?

BRECHT: Well, I must say this confirms my worst fears about you. Now I know why, even though you're a talented man, your work is so detestable.

HORVÁTH: Oh?

BRECHT: It's this disgusting passivity. You people don't understand that in the theatre it's not enough just to interpret the world any more: you have to change it.

HORVÁTH: I really think you underestimate people's intelligence. They don't want blueprints, they don't want instructions. They're being told what to do all day: they don't want to come into a theatre and be told what to do all over again. They want to be told what they are.

BRECHT: That's the easy way out.

HORVÁTH: No, it's not, lies are what's easy. The truth is invariably difficult.

BRECHT: Don't start throwing metaphysics at me. This isn't the country for metaphysics. This is the funeral parlour of the spirit. You know what I'm doing here to keep myself sane? I'm preparing a version of the Communist Manifesto in hexameters. Just to be in touch with some pure reason in this hellhole, where everyone's tongue is brown and you have to be a freak to be normal.

HORVÁTH: I've never understood why a love of mankind in general should so often be accompanied by a profound dislike of the individual. Any theories? Besides, I've always been fond of freaks. Listen, you've been there, I've always wondered, what happens to transvestites in the Soviet Union?

BRECHT: I must say, this is shaping up to be one of the most eccentric defences of capitalism I've ever encountered.

You're asking for a land fit for transvestites?

HORVÁTH: Yes.

BRECHT: I see.

HORVÁTH: After all, civilization depends, does it not, on our awareness of the sufferings of others?

BRECHT: Civilization? No, that's three kinds of fork and four kinds of wine. It's a device for maintaining the bourgeoisie's sense of superiority.

HORVÁTH: No, that's snobbery, that's something different.

BRECHT: Listen, I have people to see, I can't stand here all day quibbling over vocabulary.

HORVÁTH: It's probably best if we agree to respect our differences.

BRECHT: Well, that's the most boring suggestion I've heard all week. You can respect my differences if you like. I despise yours.

HORVÁTH: I see, you like to win arguments.

BRECHT: I did, didn't I? There's certainly no point coming second.

HORVÁTH: Well, that's the American way.

BRECHT: I'm off.

(*He turns and starts moving towards the door.* HORVÁTH *points to the banner.*)

HORVÁTH: Do take that thing with you.

(*Without a word,* BRECHT *pulls down the banner, bundles it up in his arms and goes.*)

Well, that was the last I saw of him.

(*He moves downstage and the lights fade on his apartment.*)

EIGHTEEN

Lights up on HEINRICH MANN's *sitting-room.* NELLY *is slumped in an armchair. She looks terrible.* HEINRICH *looks old and exhausted.* HORVÁTH *joins them and takes a seat. They sit in silence for a moment.*

HEINRICH: I don't know, I'm at my wits' end.

HORVÁTH: I'm not quite clear, what exactly happened?

HEINRICH: She, well, you know, she, her licence . . .

NELLY: I'll tell him, shall I, as long as I'm in the room.

HEINRICH: All right.

NELLY: I was going mad here. There was someone I needed to see. Last week I went out and hired a car and drove over. On the way back I had a head-on collision at a junction. It was entirely my fault. They tested me and said I was drunk. I was. Also there was a case of wine on the back seat. Trial's on Monday.

HORVÁTH: Oh, Christ.

NELLY: They're going to send me to jail, I know it.

HORVÁTH: No.

NELLY: What do you know?

HORVÁTH: I'm sure they won't.

NELLY: It's like a jail already, this place. For me, the whole city's like a bloody great open prison. How'm I going to stand a real jail?

HORVÁTH: You mustn't jump to conclusions, Nelly.

HEINRICH: That's what I keep telling her. You mustn't jump to conclusions.

NELLY: This conclusion jumped to me.

HORVÁTH: Now, look, we just have to put our heads together, I'm sure there's all kinds of things we can do.

HEINRICH: Of course there are, any number of things.

NELLY: Don't keep repeating everything he says like a parrot, Heini, you're giving me a headache.

HEINRICH: Don't forget, my brother has the ear of the President.

NELLY: I took a lover, Ödön, he's very young.

HEINRICH: Excuse me.

(*He rises stiffly and leaves the room.* NELLY *scarcely notices his departure.*)

NELLY: I should never have come here, never. They all treat me like dirt, every one of them. Except for you, Ödön. And Heini, of course. They think I'm not good enough for him.

HORVÁTH: I'm sure that's not true.

NELLY: I was never really happy anywhere except Berlin. I didn't care what anyone did, it didn't make any difference to me, none. I just fixed the drinks and decided if I felt like it tonight. I should never have left.

HORVÁTH: Why did you?

NELLY: I never met anyone who was kind to me like Heini was. I suddenly got it into my head that was the most important thing and I just went away to find him.

HORVÁTH: I'm sure you were right.

NELLY: No. No, because kindness isn't the only thing, Ödön. It's not . . . everything, is it, sometimes it isn't enough.

HORVÁTH: I know what you mean.

NELLY: I can't do without that boy . . . even though . . . and, you know, I'd take any . . . you know what I'm saying . . . it's not that.

HORVÁTH: Yes.

NELLY: Any . . . humiliation.

HORVÁTH: Don't.

NELLY: But nothing touches . . .

HORVÁTH: Yes.

NELLY: . . . his brutality or his indifference.

HORVÁTH: Don't let it, you shouldn't, find someone else.

NELLY: There was a time, you know, when everybody, everybody wanted me . . .

HORVÁTH: I'm sure.

(*She stretches her hand out to him.*)

NELLY: Help.

(*He takes her hand. Silence. The lights dim. After a time he lets go of her hand, rises and moves downstage.*)

HORVÁTH: I couldn't. Nobody could. Before I left, Heinrich told me he'd disposed of all her sleeping pills. But she fooled him.

(*As he speaks, NELLY makes her way over to HEINRICH's desk. She pours herself a glass of water from the carafe, then opens a drawer and brings out a bottle of pills. She starts taking handfuls of them, moving quickly. When she finishes, she drops the bottle into the wastepaper basket and lies down, curling up on the stage in a foetal position.*)

And so the whole weary scene was played again. But this time with a difference.

(*As he continues, HEINRICH comes back into the room. He*

rushes over to NELLY *and drops to one knee beside her. Then, as* HORVATH's *story moves towards its climax, strobe lighting. In its harsh glare,* HEINRICH *can be seen grappling with* NELLY's *body, heaving it up and struggling across the room with it, as if in some appalling dance.*)

He bundled her into a taxi and got her to the nearest hospital. But they were very busy, as it was just before Christmas, and they didn't like the look of this shabby old foreigner, who didn't have enough money on him, and they refused to take his cheque. So he had to call another taxi and set off to another hospital, where they were regretfully forced to take the same attitude, but at least told him of a third hospital, where he might expect better luck. He'd kept the taxi waiting this time, just in case, so they were able to speed off without delay to hospital number three, where indeed they were far more helpful and were able to tell him right away that Nelly had just died.

(*The strobe cuts out.* HEINRICH *and* NELLY *vanish, and the spot isolates* HORVÁTH.)

A few weeks before, I had been to a fund-raising meeting for Roosevelt in Bel Air. Thomas Mann, who was now an American citizen, spoke. He appeared sandwiched between a conjuror who told an interminable story about a Chinese called Rosenthal and a lady ventriloquist; and was marginally less well received than either. All the same, you could tell that America had taken him to its heart. And from then on, whenever I thought about America, the two images, one seen and one imagined, rose before me: Thomas, on that white podium in that manicured garden; and Heinrich, weeping and covered with vomit, pleading with the admissions clerk in some casualty department, trying to get some attention paid to his dying wife.
(*Silence.*)

NINETEEN

HORVÁTH: Well. The war was over.

(*He looks up.*)

We lost.

(*Pause.*)

And those of us who by chance had not been murdered had to consider whether or not we should go home and try to make our peace with those who, by chance, had not murdered us.

Most of us drifted into staying. By now, I had worked my way to the top of the hill, to a small pink stucco rancho-style cabana. I even had a minute swimming pool or waterhole, in which it was necessary to swim in circles. Also, I still loved America. Despite everything, I was still devoted to its tragic innocence.

However, the wave of post-war optimism which buoyed us up was soon to break. All over Hollywood, supporters of liberal causes, of War effort and our glorious Ally began to discover, often to their own amazement, that they were in fact premature anti-Fascists, fifth columnists, Red stooges, subversives, or even (*he whispers the word*) Communists!

(*Over this last sentence, 'America the Beautiful': however, within two bars it segues disconcertingly into the 'Internationale'. HORVÁTH grins wolfishly.*)

Opportunists crawled out of the woodwork! Buffoonish sub-committees proliferated! Idealists went to the wall! Nixon was invented! (*Quieter*) And my taste for the bizarre and ridiculous was gratified to the full.

(*The music stops.*)

Naturally, one of the first to be summoned before the House Un-American Activities Committee was . . .

(*Spot on BRECHT, wreathed in cigar smoke.*)

Bertolt Brecht.

(*Here the questions are from the recording of the actual hearing on 30 October 1947.*)

VOICE OF ROBERT E. STRIPLING: Mr Brecht, did you ever make application to join the Communist Party?

BRECHT: Er, I do not understand, er . . . the quest . . . er, the question. Did I make . . .?

VOICE OF ROBERT E. STRIPLING: Have you ever made application to join the Communist Party of any country?

BRECHT: (*Interrupting*) No, no, no, no, no, no, never.

(*The spot on* BRECHT *snaps out.*)

HORVÁTH: Well, that fooled them. The following day, he left America for good, flew back to Europe and entered into his kingdom.

Thomas Mann was also to feel hounded out eventually by McCarthyite stupidities; he chose to return to Switzerland where he could supervise the destiny of European culture from an appropriate height.

As for Heinrich, he was invited back to East Germany to be President of the German Academy of Arts. I wanted to say goodbye to him, so I drove out to Santa Monica, to the tiny apartment they'd found for him after Nelly died. I found him in the grip of a singular delusion.

TWENTY

Lights up on HEINRICH MANN's *small bed-sitting-room.* HEINRICH, *who's now seventy-eight, has aged shockingly since we last saw him. Still, he seems in good enough spirits.* HORVÁTH *joins him.*

HEINRICH: Of course, the position is largely honorary, but there will be a great many official duties. I'm rather dreading that side of it.

HORVÁTH: I'm sure it won't be that bad.

HEINRICH: Still, it's not a thing one turns down: to be President of East Germany.

HORVÁTH: I thought . . .

(*He cuts himself off, as* HEINRICH *turns to him.*)

HEINRICH: They wanted me to stand in the 1932 elections, you know, against Hitler and Hindenburg. I refused. I didn't think writers had any business meddling in politics. I was wrong. . . . So this time I really must take up the challenge.

HORVÁTH: Yes, I see that.

HEINRICH: They tell me I'm a millionaire now. Only in East German marks, but still. Nice to die a millionaire.

HORVÁTH: Yes.

HEINRICH: Only thing that worries me is having to work with Ulbricht. Awful servile little creep. You'd be sitting around a table with him and all of a sudden he'd announce it wasn't a table, it was a duckpond. And the little bugger wouldn't let you go home until you finally agreed that yes, looked at from a certain angle, you had to admit it was very like a duckpond.

HORVÁTH: Now he's Party Chairman . . .

HEINRICH: He'll be completely unbearable.

(*They smile. Then a shadow crosses* HEINRICH's *face.*)

I've been getting those émigré dreams again.

HORVÁTH: Oh, what are yours?

HEINRICH: You know, waking up in Berlin, being recognized, arrested, dragged off . . .

HORVÁTH: Mine are always Vienna: can't speak the language any more, pockets full of American money, can't remember where anything is . . .

HEINRICH: I'm frightened about going back.

HORVÁTH: That's understandable.

HEINRICH: I told you about my wife, my first wife and daughter?

HORVÁTH: Yes . . .

HEINRICH: They put them in a concentration camp, you know. Just for being my wife and daughter, no other reason.

HORVÁTH: I know.

HEINRICH: Mimi died soon after they let them out, but my daughter . . . those years, all those years in Theresienstadt, what am I going to say to her when I see her?

(*Silence.*)

HORVÁTH: I'm sure she couldn't possibly blame you.

HEINRICH: How was it we were so lucky? Something else I keep seeing in my dreams, all those queues, all those queues of desperate people outside the consulates in Marseilles. Waiting all day and then turned away. Why didn't that happen to us? I mean, what's so special about writers?

87

HORVÁTH: I don't know. I don't know.

(*Silence.*)

HEINRICH: All the people I've loved most, you know, life was too
hard for all of them. Both my sisters, Nelly, my nephew Klaus,
they all killed themselves. Why do you suppose that is?

(HORVÁTH *is groping for an answer.* HEINRICH *goes on without
waiting.*)

Most extraordinary thing, did I ever tell you? When my
sister Carla died. At the time she was the person who
meant most to me in the world. I was out walking in the
Tyrol, when I suddenly heard her calling out to me, clear as a
bell. Heinrich, Heinrich. When I got back to the hotel,
there was a telegram. She'd taken enough cyanide to kill a
company of soldiers. I know I heard her voice. Hard to
believe, but I promise you it's true.

HORVÁTH: No, I find it very easy to believe.

HEINRICH: Since then seems my whole life has been like that.
To hear people crying out from distant countries. And
nothing I could do about it.

(*Silence.*)

I think Nelly would have been all right if she'd stayed in
Europe. But, she couldn't, of course; she was frightened
they'd find out she was Jewish.

HORVÁTH: What?

HEINRICH: Oh, yes, Kröger, he was only her stepfather. Real
father was a man called Noa Troplowitz. Galician Jew.

(*Silence.* HORVÁTH *shakes his head, amazed. Very quietly, the
music:* 'Und Sonst Gar Nichts'.)

I'd left her, we'd said goodbye, she was a lovely, painful
memory. I was working in my study in Bandol-sur-mer, the
afternoon sun on my desk, when I heard a sound behind
me, in the room. I turned round and she was there. She'd
got out through Denmark, then all the way down to
France. Saved all the money out of, I don't know, tips.
And I wasn't a young man, then. It's the most beautiful
thing anyone's ever done for me.

(*He stops talking, staring ahead of him. After a moment,*
HORVÁTH *rises and moves downstage.*)

HORVÁTH: He talked to me about her for an hour or so and then I left. I felt a dull ache, as if I'd lost something I'd never owned.

(*As* HORVÁTH *continues to talk,* HEINRICH *gets up and crosses to a large wardrobe, which he opens. It's full of women's clothes. He runs a hand along them, pausing every now and then. Finally, he selects* NELLY's *red blouse. He takes it over to the bed and lays it out gently. Then he kneels by the bed and buries his face in the blouse. Eventually, he's still, his arms outstretched, his cheek against the blouse, his eyes unfocused. The lights slowly fade on this image.*)

He never got back to Europe. A couple of weeks later he spent an evening listening to Puccini—divine Puccini—went to bed and never woke up.

Thomas Mann's son-in-law called the thirties 'a low, dishonest decade'; but the fifties, which we were now embarked upon, looked worse. Blacklisting, far from being, as I had supposed, a passing phenomenon, became institutionalized; and our American colleagues began to be faced with the same choices which had tormented us in Europe before the war.

TWENTY-ONE

As he finishes speaking, HELEN SCHWARTZ *wanders disconsolately into the circle of light.* HORVÁTH *puts his arm around her. Lights up on* HELEN's *apartment.* HORVÁTH *leads* HELEN *gently into the room. She looks shattered and confused. She's formally dressed: a suit and hat.* HORVÁTH *busies himself fixing her a large scotch and ice. She looks around as if uncertain whether to sit down; finally she takes off her hat and throws it down on a chair.* HORVÁTH *hands her the drink and she takes a big slug. A moment's silence, except for the clink of the ice caused by the trembling of her hand.*

HORVÁTH: All over.
HELEN: Yes, you said it.

(*She takes another swallow of scotch.*)

HORVÁTH: Aren't you relieved?

HELEN: I guess so. But all those days and nights preparing myself and getting more and more terrified, and then to be in and out in two minutes. As long as they're going to destroy your career, I'd've thought the least they could do was put a little effort into it. It's kind of insulting when they make it so obvious how insignificant they think you are.

HORVÁTH: It's not that. It's just they are bored with people taking the Fifth. You heard the others: I refuse to answer this question on the ground it might incriminate me. They don't want to listen to this all day.

HELEN: Then they ought to mind their own fucking business.

HORVÁTH: Sure. Of course.

(*Silence.* HELEN *sits down. She puts her glass down. Finally she speaks in a small, flat voice.*)

HELEN: I'm never going to work again.

(HORVÁTH *kneels in front of her and takes her in his arms. Tears start to roll down her face, but she makes no sound.*)

HORVÁTH: Of course you are.

HELEN: No. Listen, Twentieth didn't even wait to see how it turned out. Soon as they heard I got a subpoena, they fired me.

HORVÁTH: They must have known you weren't going to name names.

HELEN: Jesus, how could anyone do that? How could they?

HORVÁTH: To keep the pool, the maid, the subscription to the golf club, the wife.

HELEN: But to inform on your friends. Jesus.

(*He kisses her.*)

HORVÁTH: I admire so much what you did. So brave.

(*He gets up and paces around for a moment.*)

What are you going to do now?

HELEN: I don't know.

HORVÁTH: Are you going to go back East?

HELEN: Why?

(*Pause. She looks at him.*)

You're all I've got now.

(*He looks away. Long silence.*)

HORVÁTH: What you did today. I . . .

(*He breaks off.*)

HELEN: Yes?

HORVÁTH: I compare it with myself and . . .

HELEN: What do you mean?

HORVÁTH: Listen, there is something, all this time, I never told you.

(HELEN *looks at him.*)

HELEN: Don't.

(HORVÁTH *nods gravely.*)

HORVÁTH: Yes, I must.

(*He takes a deep breath.*)

In 1934 I joined the German Writers' Union.

HELEN: Well, I don't see what . . .

(*She breaks off: her expression changes.*)

In 1934?

HORVÁTH: That's right. I should say the Nazi Writers' Union.

HELEN: I . . . don't understand. Why?

HORVÁTH: If you wanted to get work or to be published, you had to join.

HELEN: Oh, I see.

HORVÁTH: No, because it was not only this. I had to swear an oath that not even one of my grandparents was Jewish. I had to be certified . . . politically unobjectionable.

HELEN: You don't have to tell me all this.

HORVÁTH: No, I must get this right, it was more than this. I had to find witnesses, what you call them, references, to say I was politically reliable. One I asked was this old cretin professor who had written a book: *Adolf Hitler: Progress through Will-Power.* He signed. He said I was . . . most suitable.

(*Silence.*)

So, my boot also was on your people's faces.

(*Long silence.*)

Only thing I can say in my defence, I never paid the dues.

(*Neither of them smiles.*)

I was in two and a half years before they threw me out, and in all that time, nothing I wrote was worth shit.

HELEN: I don't understand how you could want to do that.

HORVÁTH: Did you read *Death in Venice*?

HELEN: Yes, of course.

HORVÁTH: It was a little like this, I could not leave the plague-infested city. But it was not beauty and innocence which kept me . . . enthralled, it was the grotesque, the triumph of stupidity, the ugliness.

(*Silence.*)

But no, there are no excuses.

(*Pause.*)

I should have told you before.

(HELEN *shakes her head.*)

Years, since years this has been a stone in my heart.

(HELEN *gets up and moves uncertainly around the room for a moment. Then she goes over, sits next to* HORVÁTH *and takes hold of his arm.*)

HELEN: It won't make any difference.

HORVÁTH: It will.

(*She shakes her head again and kisses him. He holds her close for a moment.*)

Yes it will.

(*Slowly he detaches himself from her and moves downstage as the lights fade on* HELEN.)

It did. A month later she left for New York but she'd already travelled further away from me than the width of a continent.

TWENTY-TWO

HORVÁTH: For me, now, Los Angeles had become a city of ghosts: and I was suddenly aware that, just as before, I was standing by and watching the poison spread. Also, I found I was starting my thirteenth year in Hollywood, and I've always been a prey to superstition. And I wanted to work in the theatre again; by now I had four unperformed plays in my desk drawer.

However.

As I was making the arrangements to go back to Europe, I was offered a job. Nothing very interesting of course, just the sequel to a dull but surprisingly successful comedy called *Bedtime for Bonzo*—but I thought it might be better to go back home with a full pocket rather than a half-empty one. Just to be on the safe side, I consulted Dieterle's astrologer. He swore by her. When I put the situation to her, she became extremely agitated. I must take the job, she said. Otherwise I would miss the greatest experience of my life. Well, I'd heard all that before, but I never could resist it.

The day of the meeting I got up early. The dawn chorus was on strike, except for a single warbling blackleg. The smog, a wartime innovation, hung low this morning, in snot-green stripes across the valley. My old Studebaker had broken down again, so I summoned a taxi to take me to Bel Air. I arrived late.

(*Lights up. Poolside. Garden of a Bel Air mansion.* ART NICELY *sits waiting in a canvas chair, an expression of well-bred impatience on his patrician features. He's about fifty, tanned, slim and manicured, tight grey curls, T-shirt and bathing shorts. He gets up as* HORVÁTH *comes stumping towards him across the lawn. They shake hands. He waves* HORVÁTH *to a chair.* HORVÁTH *sits, takes his hat off and drops it on the ground.*)

Sorry I'm late.

(NICELY *waves a hand dismissively, sits.*)

I made the mistake I got the driver to drop me at the front gate.

NICELY: Oh, you have had a walk.

HORVÁTH: Yes.

NICELY: Did you see the Renoirs on your way through the house?

HORVÁTH: No, I didn't, are they here?

NICELY: No, no, paintings, the paintings.

HORVÁTH: Oh. No.

NICELY: They're kind of fun. Look at them later.

HORVATH: Yes.

(*Silence.* NICELY *steals a look at his watch.*)

NICELY: Well. Did you have time to give our project a little thought?

HORVÁTH: Sure.

NICELY: Any ideas? I know writing a sequel isn't as interesting as doing an original, but there's a kind of discipline in it, you know?

HORVÁTH: Yes.

NICELY: OK. Let's have it.

HORVÁTH: Well, I thought . . . I mean, I was thinking about it quite a lot, to find a different direction or so, and I think what we should do in this one is we should see him . . . he should fall in love with the chimpanzee.

(*Silence.* NICELY *looks at him, perplexed.*)

NICELY: Are you serious?

HORVÁTH: Sure.

NICELY: Fall in love with the goddam chimpanzee?

HORVÁTH: Yes. This is my most interesting idea.

NICELY: Well, Ed, I don't deny it's interesting. A little too interesting I would think for the Front Office.

HORVÁTH: Don't worry. I make everything all right in the end.

NICELY: How?

HORVÁTH: Well: he marries the chimpanzee.

(NICELY *bursts out laughing.* HORVÁTH *smiles.*)

NICELY: You don't really want to do this picture, do you?

HORVÁTH: No.

NICELY: I don't blame you.

HORVÁTH: On the other hand, I need the money.

(*Silence.* NICELY *looks at his watch again, this time openly.*)

NICELY: Let me see what I can do. You want a swim?

HORVÁTH: What?

NICELY: I'm afraid I have to go now. Would you like a swim?

HORVÁTH: OK, sure, my pool's so small I only get to swim with one arm.

NICELY: Everything's in the pool house. Oh. How long do you need?

HORVÁTH: Er, twenty minutes, half an hour.

NICELY: OK, I'll send my chauffeur out for you in half an hour.
He'll take you wherever you want to go.

HORVÁTH: Thank you.

NICELY: Good to see you. I'll be in touch.

(*He shakes hands with* HORVÁTH *again and sets off across the lawn. The light begins to change to the underwater effect from the beginning of the play and to concentrate in a spot on* HORVÁTH.)

HORVÁTH: Well, I felt a bit of a fool, tell you the truth. But I was hot and it was a lovely pool, so I solemnly changed in the pool house and lowered myself gently in.

(*As he continues, the* YOUNG MAN *from the first scene of the play appears way downstage. He's wearing a black uniform and has a peaked cap under his arm. Moving with great deliberation, he puts the cap on then brings out some dark glasses, which he settles on his nose, and slowly buttons on a pair of black leather gloves. Eventually, he begins to move towards the centre of the stage.*)

I splashed about a bit and then decided to do some serious swimming. But I hadn't done more than two or three lengths, when I ran head first smack into a corner of the marble steps which led down into the centre of the pool. Everything went black. Later, there were violent struggles. I was aware of a great gash which had opened above one temple. Then, all of a sudden, through the blue-green rectangle above, I had a distorted glimpse of the rolling lawns, the obedient trees, the imposing ivy-covered walls, Eden paid for out of other men's dreams. A great peace stole over me. By the time the chauffeur arrived, looking as if he'd escaped from that new Cocteau picture, I was lying, comfortable as could be, on the bottom. The sun blazed down on us and on this Biblical city. As for me, dear friends, as for me, I was dead at last.

(*The spotlight snaps off. The* YOUNG MAN *stands, looking down into the pool. His expression remains calm. Slow fade to black.*)